# Entrepreneurship

21st CENTURY BUSINESS

SECOND EDITION

## Cynthia L. Greene

D1569254

SOUTH-WESTERN
CENGAGE Learning

Australia • Brazil • Japan • Korea • Mexico • Singapore • Spain • United Kingdom • United States

SOUTH-WESTERN
CENGAGE Learning·

**21st Century Business
Entrepreneurship, 2nd Edition**
Cynthia L. Greene

Editorial Director: Jack W. Calhoun

Vice President/Editor-in-Chief: Karen Schmohe

Executive Editor: Eve Lewis

Senior Developmental Editor: Penny Shank

Editorial Assistant: Anne Kelly

Marketing Manager: Diane Morgan

Technology Project Manager: Lysa Kosins

Content Project Management: Pre-Press PMG

Senior Manufacturing Buyer: Kevin Kluck

Production Service: Pre-Press PMG

Senior Art Director: Tippy McIntosh

Internal Design: Pre-Press PMG

Cover Designer: Lou Ann Thesing

Cover Image: Getty Images, Media Bakery

Permission Acquisitions Manager/Text:
  Mardell Glinkski-Schultz

Permission Acquisitions Manager/Photo:
  Deanna Ettinger

For product information and technology assistance, contact us at
**Cengage Learning Customer & Sales Support, 1-800-354-9706**

For permission to use material from this text or product,
submit all requests online at **www.cengage.com/permissions**
Further permissions questions can be emailed to
**permissionrequest@cengage.com**

Library of Congress Control Number: 2010920031

Student Edition ISBN 13: 978-0-538-74063-0

Student Edition ISBN 10: 0-538-74063-9

**South-Western Cengage Learning**
5191 Natorp Boulevard
Mason, OH 45040
USA

Cengage Learning products are represented in Canada by
Nelson Education, Ltd.

For your course and learning solutions, visit **cengage.com/school**

Printed in the United States of America
3 4 5 6 7 16 15 14

The *21st Century Business Series* is an innovative instructional program providing instructors with the greatest flexibility to deliver business content using a modular format. Instructors can create their own business courses by combining several **Learner Guides** in the *Series* to form one-semester or two-semester courses. The individual **Learner Guides** can also be used as enhancements to more traditional business courses or to tailor new courses to meet emerging needs.

The design and content of each **Learner Guide** in the *21st Century Business Series* are engaging yet easy for students to use. The content focuses on providing opportunities for applying 21st Century business skills while enabling innovative learning methods that integrate the use of supportive technology and creative problem-solving approaches in today's business world.

The *Entrepreneurship* **Learner Guide** covers today's most relevant business topics including the role of entrepreneurship in the global economic recovery. Topical data on how to conduct research and the important value of research as a part of entrepreneurship are also included.

# ORGANIZED FOR SUCCESS

Each chapter opens with a **Project** that incorporates information from each lesson within the chapter. These **Projects** pull all of the information from the chapter together so students get a hands-on experience applying what they learned, making for a great group activity.

**Jump Start** provides a scenario that introduces and entices the student about the lesson ahead.

## PROJECT | Identify a Business Opportunity

### Project Objectives

· Identify your strengths and weaknesses
· Determine a business opportunity that matches your strengths and weaknesses
· Use the problem-solving model to make decisions

### Getting Started

Read the Project Process below. Make a list of any materials you will need.
· Think about your interests, strengths, and weaknesses.
· Think of business opportunities that relate to your interests.

### Project Process

**1.1** Write a short paragraph describing how an individual became a successful entrepreneur.

**1.2** List all your interests. List business ideas that relate to each interest. List your strengths and weaknesses. Compare them with your list of business ideas. Cross out ideas that do not suit your strengths and weaknesses.

**1.3** Choose one of the remaining business ideas that most interests you. Set financial goals for a five-year period based on the business idea you chose. Demonstrate that your goals are SMART (Specific, Measurable, Attainable, Realistic, and Timely). Next, set nonfinancial goals you hope to achieve with this business. Be sure to include specific activities for each goal.

**1.4** Consider a problem that could occur in the business that you have chosen. Use the six-step problem-solving model to deal with it now.

### Chapter Review

**Project Wrap-up** Working with your chosen business idea, answer the six questions listed under "Compare Different Opportunities" on pages 19–20.

### 1.2 IS ENTREPRENEURSHIP RIGHT FOR YOU?

#### JUMP START

Gloria and Delia are excited about starting their own business, but before proceeding, Gloria realizes they need to slow down and think through the process carefully. "You know, Delia, it's not really easy to start our own business. When we talked about this in class, Mr. Riviera said that there are many things to consider before starting a business. First, we need to decide what we like to do and what we are good at. Then we have to do a lot of research and planning if we want to be successful." Thinking about what Mr. Riviera said in class, Delia sighs. "This entrepreneur thing sounds like a lot of work. What do you think we should do?" Why is it a good idea for Gloria and Delia to slow down and really examine their interests before starting a business?

#### GOALS

Identify the characteristics of successful entrepreneurs

Identify the characteristics of good team members

Assess whether you have what it takes to succeed in your own business

#### KEY TERMS

self-assessment, p. 13
aptitude, p. 14

#### Characteristics of Successful Entrepreneurs

Many people dream of running their own businesses. They would like to become entrepreneurs. Entrepreneurship can be exciting, but many go into it not realizing how difficult it is to run their own business. In fact, statistics show that most new businesses will fail within a few years. Startup businesses fail because of the owner's poor planning, lack of business knowledge, lack of entrepreneurial characteristics, inability to work with others, or failure to choose the right business.

1.2 Is Entrepreneurship Right for You? **11**

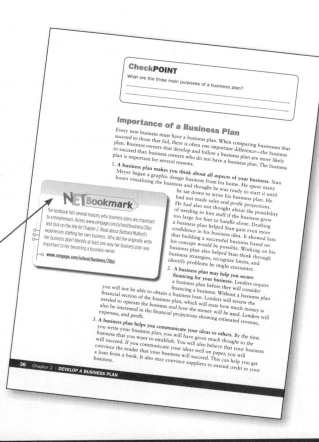

#### CheckPOINT
What are the three main purposes of a business plan?

#### Importance of a Business Plan

Every new business must have a business plan. When comparing businesses that succeed to those that fail, there is often one important difference—the business plan. Business owners that develop and follow a business plan are more likely to succeed than business owners who do not have a business plan. The business plan is important for several reasons.

1. **A business plan makes you think about all aspects of your business.** Stan Meyer began a graphic design business from his home. He spent many hours visualizing the business and thought he was ready to start it until he sat down to write his business plan. He had not made sales and profit projections. He had also not thought about the possibility of needing to hire staff if the business grew too large for him to handle alone. Drafting a business plan helped Stan gain even more confidence in his business idea. It showed him that building a successful business based on his concept would be possible. Working on his business plan also helped Stan think through business strategies, recognize limits, and identify problems he might encounter.

2. **A business plan may help you secure financing for your business.** Lenders require a business plan before they will consider financing a business. Without a business plan you will not be able to obtain a business loan. Lenders will review the financial section of the business plan, which will state how much money is needed to operate the business and how the money will be used. Lenders will also be interested in the financial projections showing estimated revenue, expenses, and profit.

3. **A business plan helps you communicate your ideas to others.** By the time you write your business plan, you will have given much thought to the business that you want to establish. You will also believe that your business will succeed. If you communicate your ideas well on paper, you will convince the reader that your business will succeed. This can help you get a loan from a bank. It also may convince suppliers to extend credit to your business.

**36** Chapter 2 · DEVELOP A BUSINESS PLAN

#### NET Bookmark

The textbook lists several reasons why business plans are important to entrepreneurs. Access www.cengage.com/school/business/21biz and click on the link for Chapter 2. Read about Barbara Mulford's experiences starting her own business. Why did she originally write her business plan? Identify at least one way her business plan was important to her becoming a business owner.

www.cengage.com/school/business/21biz

**Net Bookmark** gives chapter-related activities for students to complete using information found on the Internet.

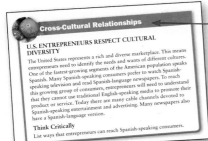

### Cross-Cultural Relationships

**U.S. ENTREPRENEURS RESPECT CULTURAL DIVERSITY**

The United States represents a rich and diverse marketplace. This means entrepreneurs need to identify the needs and wants of different cultures. One of the fastest-growing segments of the American population speaks Spanish. Many Spanish-speaking consumers prefer to watch Spanish-speaking television and read Spanish-language newspapers. To reach this growing group of consumers, entrepreneurs will need to understand that they cannot use traditional English-speaking media to promote their product or service. Today there are many cable channels devoted to Spanish-speaking entertainment and advertising. Many newspapers also have a Spanish-language version.

**Think Critically**
List ways that entrepreneurs can reach Spanish-speaking consumers.

**Cross-Cultural Relationships** highlights the importance of understanding and respecting everyone's point of view and thinking about the perspectives of others.

**Teamwork** provides an activity that requires students to work together as a team.

### Tech Literacy

**PREPARING THE BUSINESS PLAN**
There are many software programs available for entrepreneurs to use when preparing a business plan. A recent Internet search showed more than 345,000 matches for "business plan software." Many entrepreneurs use these programs because they provide an easy-to-use template. By plugging your specific information into the template, you get a professional-looking finished report. If you decide to use a software program to create your business plan, be sure it includes all of the essential elements. It is a good idea to evaluate several different programs before deciding which one to use. Your choice should best match the information you want to include and your desired style. And, of course, it should be one that you can use without difficulty.

**THINK CRITICALLY**
What are some of the advantages and disadvantages of using business plan software?

**Tech Literacy** highlights how evolving technology plays a huge role in how business is conducted.

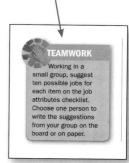

**TEAMWORK**
Working in a small group, suggest ten possible jobs for each item on the job attributes checklist. Choose one person to write the suggestions from your group on the board or on paper.

### Enter a Family Business

The United States economy is dominated by family businesses. According to some estimates, as many as 90 percent of all businesses, including the vast majority of small- and medium-sized companies, are owned by families. Even many large companies, such as Chick-fil-A, continue to be owned and operated largely by people who are related to the company founder.

**DID YOU KNOW ?**
According to the University of Southern Maine's Institute for Family-Owned Business, 35 percent of Fortune 500 companies are family-controlled. Family businesses account for 50 percent of U.S. gross domestic product. They generate 60 percent of U.S. employment and 78 percent of all new job creation.

### Advantages of a Family Business

Entrepreneurs who work for their family businesses enjoy the pride and sense of mission that comes with being part of a family enterprise. They also enjoy the fact that their businesses remain in the family for at least one more generation. Some enjoy working with relatives. They also like knowing that their efforts are benefiting others whom they care about.

### Disadvantages of a Family Business

Family businesses have several drawbacks. Senior management positions are often held by family members, regardless of their ability. This situation sometimes means that poor business decisions are made. It also makes it difficult to retain good employees who are not members of the family. Family politics often enter into business decision making. Plus, the distinction between business life and private life is blurred in family-owned businesses. As a result, business problems end up affecting family life as well.

*If you are not a family member, why might it be difficult to work in a family-owned business?*

Entrepreneurs who do join their family business must be prepared to make compromises. Unlike those who start or buy their own companies, people who work for their families lack the freedom to make all decisions themselves. They may also be unable to set policies and procedures as they would like.

### CheckPOINT

What are some of the advantages and disadvantages of entering a family business?

You will find the following features throughout each chapter:

- **Did You Know?** always focuses on valuable and interesting data relevant to today's business world.

- **CheckPOINT** where students can jot down answers to important questions as they go through the lessons in the chapter.

- **Think Critically** is part of the lesson assessment where students answer questions with information that was provided in the preceding lesson.

### Think Critically

1. Why do you think the quality of the business plan is so critical to an entrepreneur's success?

2. Melinda Rosati wants to purchase her uncle's barbershop. Because it is an ongoing business, Melinda doesn't think she needs to write a business plan. Do you agree or disagree with Melinda's opinion? Why or why not?

3. Putting your business plan in writing helps you communicate your ideas to others. Do you think discussing your business plan out loud in a meeting can also help you get your ideas across? Why or why not?

## CHAPTER 4

# Market Your Business

**4.1** The Value of Marketing

**4.2** Create the Marketing Plan

**4.3** Identify Your Competition

**4.4** The Marketing Mix—Product and Price

**4.5** The Marketing Mix—Distribution and Promotion

86

### Careers for Entrepreneurs

*Marketing*

**LRMR**

LeBron James is not content with just being a star on the basketball court. He also wants to become a leader in the global business world. He formed a sports marketing agency, LRMR Innovative Marketing and Branding, with three of his high school friends. In addition to turning James into a global icon, LRMR wants to "change the sports marketing prism through leveraging of sports, celebrity, and corporate infusion partnerships."

James wants to build a new financial model for the 21st-century athlete. He also formed King James, Inc., a holding company, to contract with endorsement partners and reduce tax liability.

Guiding principles that James has used in starting his business include
• Don't be afraid to ask for business advice
• Focus on unity rather than the individual
• Surround yourself with the best people
• Diversify income streams
• Remember that the brand is bigger than the man

**Think Critically**
1. What do you think contributes to the success of LRMR?
2. Identify trends that you think could influence the success of LRMR.

---

Each chapter starts out with a **"Careers for Entrepreneurs"** feature that focuses on a real business and reflects one of the 16 Career Clusters.

---

Throughout the book, you will find **Business Math Connection**. This feature highlights how basic math concepts are an important part of the business world.

---

### Price a Product

Once pricing objectives have been determined, the next step is to determine the possible prices for products. There will usually be more than one price that can be charged for a product. Pricing may be based on demand, cost, or the amount of competition.

**Demand-Based Pricing** Pricing that is determined by how much customers are willing to pay for a product or service is called *demand-based pricing*. Potential customers are surveyed to find out what they would be willing to pay. The highest price identified is the maximum price that can be charged.

**Cost-Based Pricing** Pricing that is determined by using the wholesale cost of an item as the basis for the price charged is called *cost-based pricing*. A *markup price* is the retail price determined by adding a percentage amount to the wholesale cost of an item.

Sometimes business owners purchase too much of a particular item and want to sell more of it quickly. To do so, they mark down the retail price of the product. A *markdown price* is a price determined by subtracting a percentage amount from the retail price of an item. You should be careful not to mark down an item below its cost. You do not want to lose money.

**Competition-Based Pricing** Pricing that is determined by considering what competitors charge for the same good or service is called *competition-based pricing*. Once you find out what your competition charges for an item, you must decide whether to charge the same price, slightly more, or slightly less.

#### Business Math Connection

If Luisa Ramirez, a gourmet food store owner, buys artichoke hearts for $1.77 a can and wants to add 40 percent to the wholesale cost, what would the retail (markup) price be? If Luisa usually sells olive oil for $10.50 a bottle and wants to mark down the price 20 percent to try to sell more olive oil, what would the markdown price be?

**SOLUTION**
Use the following formulas to calculate retail price.

| Wholesale cost | × | Percentage markup | = | Markup amount |
|---|---|---|---|---|
| $1.77 | × | 0.40 | = | $0.71 |

| Wholesale cost | + | Markup amount | = | Retail price |
|---|---|---|---|---|
| $1.77 | + | $0.71 | = | $2.48 |

Use the following formulas to calculate markdown price.

| Retail price | × | Percentage markdown | = | Markdown amount |
|---|---|---|---|---|
| $10.50 | × | 0.20 | = | $2.10 |

| Retail price | − | Markdown amount | = | Markdown price |
|---|---|---|---|---|
| $10.50 | − | $2.10 | = | $8.40 |

110 Chapter 4 · MARKET YOUR BUSINESS

---

## MARKET RESEARCH SURVEY

*Thank you for participating in this market research survey. We appreciate your assistance in helping us identify the needs of pet owners in our community.*

**PLEASE CHECK THE BOX THAT BEST DESCRIBES YOUR SITUATION.**

Age: UNDER 18 ☐  19–30 ☐  31–40 ☐  41–50 ☐  51–65 ☐  OVER 65 ☐

Gender: MALE ☐  FEMALE ☐

Annual Household Income:

LESS THAN $25,000 ☐  $25,000–$50,000 ☐  $50,001–$100,000 ☐  MORE THAN $100,000 ☐

Number of pets: 0 ☐  1 ☐  2 ☐  3 ☐  4 OR MORE ☐

Kinds of pets: DOG ☐  CAT ☐  FISH ☐  BIRD ☐  OTHER ☐ (PLEASE SPECIFY)

IF YOU OWN A DOG, PLEASE ANSWER ALL OF THE FOLLOWING QUESTIONS.

How often do you walk your dog?

EVERY DAY ☐  A FEW TIMES A WEEK ☐  ONLY ON THE WEEKENDS ☐  NEVER ☐

OTHER ☐ (PLEASE SPECIFY)

Would you be willing to pay someone you trusted to take your dog for walks?

YES ☐  POSSIBLY ☐  NO ☐

How much would you be willing to pay to have your dog(s) walked for 30 minutes?

$10 ☐  $15 ☐  $20 ☐  $25 ☐  I WOULD NOT PAY TO HAVE MY DOG WALKED ☐

Who takes care of your dog when you are out of town?

KENNEL ☐  FRIEND ☐  NEIGHBOR ☐  OTHER ☐ (PLEASE SPECIFY)

Would you be interested in having someone you trust take care of your pets while you are away?

YES ☐  POSSIBLY ☐  NO ☐

4.2 Create the Marketing Plan  97

### COMMUNICATE

Call your local Chamber of Commerce and ask them for information that would help the owner of a new dog-walking business that is opening in your town or city. Do not forget information on demographics and psychographics. Also, ask for statistics on dog ownership in your area. Write a report on your findings and present it to your class.

---

**Communicate** is an activity to reinforce, review, and practice communication skills.

# HANDS-ON LEARNING

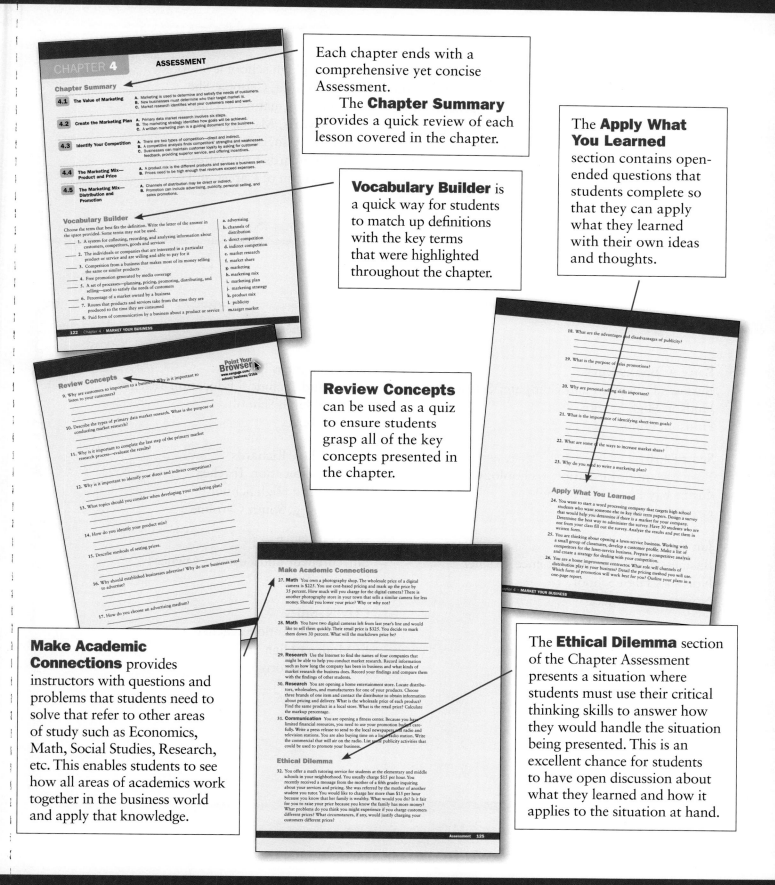

Each chapter ends with a comprehensive yet concise Assessment.
The **Chapter Summary** provides a quick review of each lesson covered in the chapter.

**Vocabulary Builder** is a quick way for students to match up definitions with the key terms that were highlighted throughout the chapter.

The **Apply What You Learned** section contains open-ended questions that students complete so that they can apply what they learned with their own ideas and thoughts.

**Review Concepts** can be used as a quiz to ensure students grasp all of the key concepts presented in the chapter.

**Make Academic Connections** provides instructors with questions and problems that students need to solve that refer to other areas of study such as Economics, Math, Social Studies, Research, etc. This enables students to see how all areas of academics work together in the business world and apply that knowledge.

The **Ethical Dilemma** section of the Chapter Assessment presents a situation where students must use their critical thinking skills to answer how they would handle the situation being presented. This is an excellent chance for students to have open discussion about what they learned and how it applies to the situation at hand.

**Cynthia L. Greene** taught business education at the high school level for 25 years in the Fulton County School System in Atlanta, Georgia. She served as the program specialist for Business and Information Technology for the Georgia Department of Education for six years. Ms. Greene is an active member of the National Business Education Association, serving as President and member of the Entrepreneurship Standards Committee. She is the business manager of the Georgia Association of Career and Technical Education.

## Reviewers

**Betty A. Banks-Burke**
Business Education and Computer Science Teacher
Hudson High School
Hudson, Ohio

**Scott Christy**
Business and Information Technology Instructor
Green Bay East High School
Green Bay, Wisconsin

**Jan Goddard**
Business and Computer Science Teacher
Norcross High School
Norcross, Georgia

**Vernon W. King, Jr.**
Marketing Education Coordinator
Landstown High School
Virginia Beach, Virginia

**Dennis R. Krejci**
Business Teacher
Tri County High School
DeWitt, Nebraska

**Katherine Jones Nance**
Career and Technical Education Teacher
Parkland High School
El Paso, Texas

**Jenifer Clary Richards**
Business Education Teacher
Spartanburg High School
Spartanburg, South Carolina

**Vickie Banks Reed**
Entrepreneur and Business Owner
Coppell, Texas

**Clay N. Stiles**
Business Education Teacher
El Modena High School
Orange, California

# CONTENTS

# Should You Become an Entrepreneur?

## Careers for Entrepreneurs

Arts, A/V Technology & Communications

### J. K. ROWLING

Ask successful people how to succeed, and they will always tell you to do what you love. For a fortunate few, that formula works. Such is the case with J. K. Rowling, creator of *Harry Potter* and one of the most successful writers in the world today.

Rowling always wanted to be a writer, but before her success came a young adulthood full of indecision. Rowling went to Exeter University and studied French. She worked as a secretary but discovered that she liked nothing about it and spent time working on stories at the computer. She was eventually fired and went abroad to teach English in Portugal. With her mornings free, she began work on her third novel after giving up on two others.

When she left Portugal, her suitcase was filled with stories about Harry Potter. She decided to finish the novel and try to get it published before starting work as a French teacher. A publisher bought the book one year after it was finished. The road to success for J. K. Rowling had begun!

### Think Critically

1. Why do many entrepreneurs have unsuccessful experiences as an employee?
2. Why do you think the *Harry Potter* books have been so successful?

## Project Objectives

- Identify your strengths and weaknesses
- Determine a business opportunity that matches your strengths and weaknesses
- Use the problem-solving model to make decisions

Photodisc/Getty Images

## Getting Started

Read the Project Process below. Make a list of any materials you will need.
- Think about your interests, strengths, and weaknesses.
- Think of business opportunities that relate to your interests.

## Project Process

**1.1** Write a short paragraph describing how an individual became a successful entrepreneur.

**1.2** List all your interests. List business ideas that relate to each interest. List your strengths and weaknesses. Compare them with your list of business ideas. Cross out ideas that do not suit your strengths and weaknesses.

**1.3** Choose one of the remaining business ideas that most interests you. Set financial goals for a five-year period based on the business idea you chose. Demonstrate that your goals are SMART (Specific, Measurable, Attainable, Realistic, and Timely). Next, set nonfinancial goals you hope to achieve with this business. Be sure to include specific activities for each goal.

**1.4** Consider a problem that could occur in the business that you have chosen. Use the six-step problem-solving model to deal with it now.

## Chapter Review

**Project Wrap-up** Working with your chosen business idea, answer the six questions listed under "Compare Different Opportunities" on pages 19–20.

Creatas/Jupiter Images

**GOALS**

Define entrepreneurship

Recognize entrepreneurial opportunities and factors for success

**KEY TERMS**

entrepreneurs, p. 4

entrepreneurship, p. 4

employees, p. 5

 **JUMP START**

John owns a house painting business. While he was shopping for painting supplies at the hardware store, he noticed a new device that would make painting around trim and other edges much easier. The design was so simple that John wondered why he hadn't thought of it. An entrepreneur is someone who takes an idea, acts on it, and develops it to offer a new product or service. Have you ever seen a new product or service and thought to yourself, "I had the same idea. I wish I had started this business!"

Photodisc/Getty Images

## What Is an Entrepreneur?

The U.S. economy includes thousands of small businesses. Many of these small businesses are owned and operated by men and women who created their own companies. What makes someone an entrepreneur? What impact have entrepreneurs had in history? What impact do they have today?

People who own, operate, and take the risk of a business venture are called **entrepreneurs**. They are engaged in **entrepreneurship**, the process of running a business of one's own. Entrepreneurs come from all types of backgrounds and create all kinds of businesses. People of all ages choose to become entrepreneurs. Some own tiny craft shops while others own huge construction companies. Entrepreneurs try to identify unmet needs in the marketplace. Then they provide a service or product to meet those needs. When they succeed, their businesses flourish and profits are earned. But if their business idea is unsuccessful, they may lose the money they invested.

## Employees vs. Entrepreneurs

Entrepreneurs assume risk. This makes them different from **employees**, who are people who work for someone else. Both may make decisions, but only the entrepreneur is directly affected by the consequences of those decisions. Sam Jones manages a record store owned by Felipe Santiago. Sam decides to keep the store open until midnight during the week. If the additional hours bring in customers and increase profits, Sam may be praised by Felipe. He may even get a raise. However, Sam won't directly receive any of the profits because he is an employee. The additional earnings will flow to Felipe, the owner.

## Why Do People Become Entrepreneurs?

People go into business for themselves for many reasons. Some want to leave the fast-paced corporate environment and set their own schedules. Others want to be at home but still earn an income. Still others want to pursue a personal dream. You might choose to become an entrepreneur for completely different reasons.

## Types of Entrepreneurial Businesses

There are generally four types of businesses, and there are opportunities for entrepreneurs in each type. See the chart on the next page. *Manufacturing businesses* actually produce the products they sell. Using resources and supplies, they create everything from automobiles to paper. *Wholesaling businesses* sell products to other businesses rather than the final consumer. For example, a wholesaler supplies your local greeting card store with items such as cards and wrapping paper. *Retailing businesses*, such as a greeting card store, sell products directly to those who use or consume them. *Service businesses* sell services rather than products. They include hotels, hairdressers, and repair shops.

**Other Business Areas** Two other categories of businesses are (1) agricultural and (2) mining and extracting businesses. *Agricultural businesses* generate fresh produce and other farm products, such as wheat. *Mining and extracting businesses* take resources like coal out of the ground so they can be consumed.

**Green Entrepreneurship** In today's economy, there are many opportunities for entrepreneurs who have ideas for new products or services that are considered green or organic. Because of the growing movement toward environmentally friendly products, entrepreneurs who have a passion toward being green have an advantage when introducing their product or service on the market. It is important for green entrepreneurs to educate their customers about how their products or services benefit the earth or conserve resources. In addition to offering green products, entrepreneurs who use green business practices, such as recycling and working with other green-minded companies, are often favored by customers.

**TEAMWORK**

Work in teams to compile a list of advantages and disadvantages of being an employee. List advantages and disadvantages of being an entrepreneur. As a class, compare and contrast the lists.

## TYPES OF ENTREPRENEURIAL BUSINESSES

| Manufacturing | Wholesaling | Retailing | Service |
|---|---|---|---|
| Apparel and other textile products | Apparel | Auto and home supply stores | Appliance repair |
| Chemicals and related products | Electrical goods | Building materials and supply stores | Automotive repair |
| Electronics and other electrical equipment | Groceries and related products | Clothing stores | Babysitting |
| Fabricated metal products | Hardware, plumbing, heating equipment | Florists | Bookkeeping |
| Food products | Lumber, construction materials | Furniture stores | Consulting |
| Industrial machinery and equipment | Machinery, equipment, supplies | Gift, novelty, and souvenir stores | Dance instruction |
| Printing and publishing | Motor vehicles, automotive equipment | Grocery stores | Exterminators |
| Rubber and miscellaneous plastic products | Paper, paper products | Hardware stores | Electrical service |
| Stone, clay, and glass products | Petroleum, petroleum products | Jewelry stores | Flower decorating |
| | | Retail bakeries | House cleaning |
| | | Shoe stores | Lawn care |
| | | Sporting goods and bicycle stores | Painting |
| | | | Plumbing |
| | | | Translating |
| | | | Travel agency |
| | | | Tutoring |
| | | | Web design and maintenance |

## CheckPOINT

Describe different types of entrepreneurial businesses.

_____

_____

_____

# Recognizing Opportunity

Many of America's most successful companies started with one person who recognized an opportunity and came up with an idea for a business in response to that opportunity. Entrepreneurs have played an important role in the history of America's economy and will continue to shape our economy in the future.

According to estimates from the U.S. Small Business Administration's Office of Advocacy, there were approximately 29.6 million businesses in the United States in 2008. Small firms with fewer than 500 employees represent 99.9 percent of these U.S. businesses. Only 18,000 U.S. businesses are considered large. According to the National Small Business Association, small businesses created 21.9 million jobs in the last 15 years compared with 1.8 million jobs for large businesses.

## Entrepreneurs Who Changed America

Entrepreneurs change American business decade after decade. They establish new companies and fill unmet needs. They continuously change how things are done and contribute to the overall economic good of the nation.

**Starbucks Coffee Company** Starbucks Coffee Company was founded in 1971, opening its first location in Seattle's Pike Place Market. Starbucks is named after the first mate in Herman Melville's novel Moby Dick. It is the world's leading brand of specialty coffee. Its stores receive more than 40 million customer visits per week at coffeehouses in North America, Europe, the Middle East, Latin America, and the Pacific Rim. When Howard Schultz first joined the company in the early 1980s, Starbucks was already a highly respected local roaster and retailer of whole bean and ground coffees. A business trip to Italy, where he was impressed with the popularity of espresso bars, helped Schultz recognize an opportunity to develop a similar coffeehouse culture in Seattle. Espresso drinks became an essential element of Schultz's vision. He purchased Starbucks with the support of local investors in 1987. In addition to its well-situated coffeehouses, Starbucks markets its coffee and tea products through its website and through many national retail supermarkets.

Why has Starbucks been so successful?

© Brendan Howard, 2009/ Used under license from Shutterstock.com

## Cross-Cultural Relationships

### U.S. ENTREPRENEURS RESPECT CULTURAL DIVERSITY

The United States represents a rich and diverse marketplace. This means entrepreneurs need to identify the needs and wants of different cultures. One of the fastest-growing segments of the American population speaks Spanish. Many Spanish-speaking consumers prefer to watch Spanish-speaking television and read Spanish-language newspapers. To reach this growing group of consumers, entrepreneurs will need to understand that they cannot use traditional English-speaking media to promote their product or service. Today there are many cable channels devoted to Spanish-speaking entertainment and advertising. Many newspapers also have a Spanish-language version.

### Think Critically

List ways that entrepreneurs can reach Spanish-speaking consumers.

**The Home Depot** In 1979, Bernie Marcus and Arthur Blank opened the first The Home Depot stores in Atlanta, Georgia, forever changing the home improvement industry. They envisioned a home improvement store that offered one-stop shopping for the do-it-yourselfers. The original stores stocked around 25,000 products. An average store today offers 40,000 products in approximately 105,000 square feet. Marcus and Blank's vision was of warehouse stores filled from floor to ceiling with a wide assortment of home improvement products at the lowest possible prices and with the best possible service. Within five years, The Home Depot expanded from Georgia to Florida, Louisiana, Texas, and Alabama. Today, it has more than 2,200 stores throughout the world.

**Harpo Productions, Inc.** Oprah Winfrey's love of acting and her desire to produce quality entertainment projects prompted her to form her own production company, HARPO Productions, Inc., in 1986. Today, HARPO is a formidable force in film and television production. Based in Chicago, HARPO Entertainment Group includes HARPO Productions, Inc., HARPO Films, and HARPO Video, Inc. In October 1988, HARPO Productions, Inc., acquired ownership and all production responsibilities for *The Oprah Winfrey Show* from Capital Cities/ABC, making Oprah Winfrey the first woman in history to own and produce her own talk show. Oprah has also produced and appeared in several television miniseries and movies.

## Entrepreneurial Opportunities in Economic Recovery

Even during downturns in the economy, entrepreneurial opportunities still exist. While big businesses tend to be more conservative in their approach to economic slowdowns by scaling back production, conserving cash, and laying off workers, small businesses that have less to lose are more willing and able to make changes quickly. They can be more creative and take more risks than large companies. Their experimentation and innovation lead to technological change and increased productivity. This makes small businesses a significant part of the economic recovery process.

The American Recovery and Reinvestment Act of 2009 was passed to stimulate the American economy after the 2008 economic slowdown. It has a number of provisions to help small businesses, including $30 billion in tax relief for small businesses and $13 billion in loans, lines of credit, and equity capital. Other provisions include

- Increasing the Small Business Administration (SBA) guarantee on loans up to 95% of loan value
- Improving the liquidity of small business lending markets
- Allowing the SBA to refinance existing loans, including those with both the SBA and other lenders
- Increasing equity capital for high-growth businesses
- Providing lending assistance for borrowers locked out of traditional financing markets
- Offering tax relief in several forms

The stimulus package also contains significant new support to increase green businesses, including incentives to drive the growth of renewable energy, stimulate energy efficiency efforts, and update the national electrical grid.

## Business Success or Failure

Although there are many opportunities for entrepreneurial success, there is also a risk of failure. According to a recent study by the Small Business Administration's Office of Advocacy, two-thirds of new businesses survive at least two years, and 44 percent survive at least four years. This means that more than half of all new businesses do not survive beyond four years. These results are similar for different industries. Many people think that there is a higher failure rate for restaurants than other types of businesses. However, leisure and hospitality establishments, which include restaurants, survive at rates only slightly below the average. Major factors in a firm's success include having adequate capital, providing a product or service that meets customer needs, the owner's education level, and the owner's reason for starting the firm in the first place, such as freedom for family life or wanting to be one's own boss. The reason must sufficiently motivate the entrepreneur to have the perseverance to succeed.

The owner's business experience is a factor that contributes to the likelihood of success. Experienced businesspeople have an understanding of how to purchase products and services. They know how to plan, negotiate with suppliers, raise money, negotiate leases, sell and market their product or service, and manage finances. Many businesses fail because the owner lacks business knowledge. Someone may have an idea for a product or service but lack the necessary business skills he or she needs to run a successful business. There is a major difference between having expertise regarding a product or service and running a business with that product or service. So when opportunity presents itself, entrepreneurs must have what it takes to succeed.

How does an owner's business experience play a role in the business's success?

## CheckPOINT

What role do small businesses play in the U.S. economy?

_____

_____

## Think Critically

1. What are your reasons for wanting to become an entrepreneur? Do you think they are common to all entrepreneurs, or are they unique?

_____

_____

2. Why do you think entrepreneurship is important to the U.S. economy? Provide specific examples of how entrepreneurs affect the economy.

_____

_____

_____

3. What do you think is the most important thing an entrepreneur should do before starting a business to help ensure its success?

_____

_____

_____

## Make Academic Connections

4. **Math** Suppose there are exactly 5,812,000 small businesses in the economy today. Approximately 27 percent of those businesses are service businesses. What is the number of service businesses in the economy? Suppose 14 percent of those service businesses close after two years. How many service businesses remain open?

_____

_____

5. **Social Studies** Before Starbucks grew nationwide, there were few places that people could go to have coffee and meet with friends and business associates. Use word processing software to compose at least one paragraph about how Starbucks and other coffee shops have changed the way people view coffee and its role in society.

6. **Communication** Entrepreneurs can be of any age. Research a teen entrepreneur. Use word processing software to write a one-page paper about his or her business. Discuss whether or not you think the business idea is a good one. Make recommendations for expanding the business.

**JUMP START**

Gloria and Delia are excited about starting their own business, but before proceeding, Gloria realizes they need to slow down and think through the process carefully. "You know, Delia, it's not really easy to start our own business. When we talked about this in class, Mr. Riviera said that there are many things to consider before starting a business. First, we need to decide what we like to do and what we are good at. Then we have to do a lot of research and planning if we want to be successful." Thinking about what Mr. Riviera said in class, Delia sighs. "This entrepreneur thing sounds like a lot of work. What do you think we should do?" Why is it a good idea for Gloria and Delia to slow down and really examine their interests before starting a business?

### GOALS

**Identify the characteristics of successful entrepreneurs**

**Identify the characteristics of good team members**

**Assess whether you have what it takes to succeed in your own business**

### KEY TERMS

**self-assessment,** p. 13

**aptitude,** p. 14

©Anton Gvozdikov, 2009/ Used under license from Shutterstock.com

## Characteristics of Successful Entrepreneurs

Many people dream of running their own businesses. They would like to become entrepreneurs. Entrepreneurship can be exciting, but many go into it not realizing how difficult it is to run their own business. In fact, statistics show that most new businesses will fail within a few years. Startup businesses fail because of the owner's poor planning, lack of business knowledge, lack of entrepreneurial characteristics, inability to work with others, or failure to choose the right business.

Researchers have identified several characteristics that distinguish successful entrepreneurs from those that fail.

1. **Successful entrepreneurs are independent.** They want to make their own decisions and do something they enjoy.

2. **Successful entrepreneurs are self-confident.** Entrepreneurs make all the decisions. They must have the confidence to make choices alone and bounce back from a poorly made decision.

3. **Successful entrepreneurs have determination and perseverance.** Entrepreneurs persist through hard times until goals are met.

4. **Successful entrepreneurs are goal-oriented.** They know what they want, and they are able to focus on achieving it.

5. **Successful entrepreneurs have a need to achieve and to set high standards for themselves.** They are motivated by setting and achieving challenging goals.

Why should entrepreneurs be goal-oriented?

6. **Successful entrepreneurs are creative.** They think of new ways to market their businesses and always look for new solutions to problems.

7. **Successful entrepreneurs are able to act quickly.** They are not afraid to make quick decisions when necessary, which helps them beat their competitors.

8. **Successful entrepreneurs keep up to date with technology.** New technologies emerge that can help with many business activities. In order to run their business efficiently, entrepreneurs should always be on the lookout for new technology they can apply to their business.

## Check**POINT**

Name three important characteristics of entrepreneurs.

_____

_____

# Characteristics of Good Team Members

Entrepreneurs realize that there are other stakeholders in their businesses—partners, investors, employees, suppliers, customers, creditors, and so forth. They must work with others to get their business up and running. They must have good team-building skills as well as be effective team members. Good team members display the following traits.

1. **Commitment**   They are committed to team goals and willing to work hard to achieve the goals.

2. **Competency**   They have the right skills needed to get the job done and to help accomplish the team's goals.

3. **Communication**   They have good communication skills and can share ideas with others in both oral and written form.

4. **Cooperation**   They must work well with others and know that they will not always get their way. They are willing to accept the decision of the group for the good of the group.

5. **Creativity**   They are able to look at things from different perspectives and suggest new ways of doing things.

## NETBookmark

Your textbook lists several characteristics of successful entrepreneurs. Do you have what it takes to be an entrepreneur? Access www.cengage.com/school/business/21biz and click on the link for Chapter 1. Take this brief online quiz to find out. What are some personal characteristics assessed by the test? Which do you think are the most relevant? Based on your personal test results, do you think you would be a successful entrepreneur?

**www.cengage.com/school/business/21biz**

## CheckPOINT

Why is it important for entrepreneurs to be good team members?

_____

_____

# Are You Right for Entrepreneurship?

Entrepreneurship is not for everyone. Some people lack the qualities needed to become successful entrepreneurs. Others lack the aptitude needed to run a business. To determine if entrepreneurship is right for you, you need to perform a self-assessment. A **self-assessment** is an evaluation of your strengths and weaknesses. You can do this in a number of ways. You can list what you believe to be your strengths and weaknesses on a sheet of paper. You can ask others what they believe your strengths are and where your weaknesses lie. There are also professional tests you can take to assess your abilities.

Why is it important to assess your strengths and weaknesses before starting a business?

## Assess Your Interests

Success as an entrepreneur requires a strong commitment to a business and a lot of energy. To be able to commit yourself fully to a business, you should choose a field that interests you and that will provide you with an experience you will enjoy. Many entrepreneurs center a business on an interest or hobby. Analyzing past experiences and jobs can also help. Building a business around jobs or experiences that you found fulfilling could lead to success.

## Assess Your Aptitude

Different jobs require different job aptitudes. **Aptitude** is the ability to learn a particular kind of job. Auto mechanics must possess an aptitude for solving mechanical problems and must be good with their hands. People who sell insurance must have good interpersonal skills. Answering questions like those in the Job Attributes Checklist can help you identify the kinds of entrepreneurial opportunities that might match your aptitudes and interests.

### TEAMWORK

Working in a small group, suggest ten possible jobs for each item on the job attributes checklist. Choose one person to write the suggestions from your group on the board or on paper.

### JOB ATTRIBUTES CHECKLIST

- ☐ 1. I enjoy working with numbers.
- ☐ 2. I enjoy working outdoors.
- ☐ 3. I enjoy working with my hands.
- ☐ 4. I enjoy selling.
- ☐ 5. I like working with people.
- ☐ 6. I prefer to work alone.
- ☐ 7. I like supervising other people.
- ☐ 8. I like knowing exactly what it is I am supposed to do.

## Assess the Advantages of Entrepreneurship

Many people see significant advantages in owning their own businesses. Some of the biggest advantages include the following.

1. **Entrepreneurs are their own bosses.** Nobody tells an entrepreneur what to do. Entrepreneurs control their own destinies.

2. **Entrepreneurs can choose a business that interests them.** Entrepreneurs work in fields that interest them. Many combine hobbies and interests with business.

3. **Entrepreneurs can be creative.** Entrepreneurs are always implementing creative ideas they think of themselves.

4. **Entrepreneurs can make large sums of money.** Entrepreneurship involves risk, but if the business is successful, the business owner will reap the profits.

Financially, what are the advantages and disadvantages of entrepreneurship?

## Assess the Disadvantages of Entrepreneurship

All prospective entrepreneurs must carefully weigh the advantages against the disadvantages before making the decision to start a business. Disadvantages include the following.

1. **Entrepreneurship is risky.** There is the possibility of losing money and going out of business.

2. **Entrepreneurs face uncertain and irregular incomes.** Entrepreneurs may make money one month and lose money the next.

3. **Entrepreneurs work long hours.** Entrepreneurs are never really finished with their jobs. They can work long, irregular hours. They receive no paid days off and often work evenings and weekends.

4. **Entrepreneurs must make all decisions by themselves.** Unless they have partners, entrepreneurs have the final responsibility for all decisions that are made regarding the business.

## Check**POINT**

What kinds of assessments should you make to determine if you are right for entrepreneurship?

_____

_____

# Think Critically

1. Entrepreneurs can fail even if they are committed and have the characteristics needed to be successful. Why do you think this can happen?

_____

_____

_____

2. What traits do good team members have? Select one trait and explain why it is important.

_____

_____

_____

3. Do you think the advantages of entrepreneurship outweigh the disadvantages? Why or why not?

_____

_____

_____

# Make Academic Connections

4. **Technology** In today's business environment, it is important that entrepreneurs keep up to date with technology. Research technology products and services that would be useful to the owner of a business. Describe one and explain how it can help business owners run their companies more efficiently.

_____

_____

_____

5. **Career Success** Choose a business idea that you think you would like. Using the Job Attributes Checklist, compare your interests and aptitudes to your business idea. Is this a good choice for you? Why or why not?

_____

_____

6. **Communication** Rank the advantages of entrepreneurship in order of importance to you. The item ranked "1" is the most important, and the item ranked "4" is the least important. Write a paragraph explaining your rankings.

**JUMP START**

Gloria and Delia realize that although there are many advantages to owning their own business, there are many challenges that a business owner faces. Gloria knows that she and Delia have their work cut out for them, but she has confidence they can do it if they put their minds to it. She also knows that they really need to have a good idea and be certain that there are people who are willing to pay them for the product or service they want to sell. "How do we decide what kind of business we should have?" Delia asks Gloria. "There are so many businesses in our community," Gloria responds. "We have to come up with just the right idea!" How do people come up with ideas for new businesses? How do you think they decide if the idea is worth pursuing?

### GOALS

**Identify sources for new business ideas**

**Evaluate different business opportunities**

**Identify your own personal goals**

### KEY TERMS

**opportunities,** p. 17

**ideas,** p. 17

**trade shows,** p. 19

©michaeljung, 2009/ Used under license from Shutterstock.com

## Look for Ideas

Millions of entrepreneurs in the United States start their own businesses. You may wonder how they decided what businesses to operate? They may have acted on a new idea or an opportunity. An idea is different from an opportunity. **Opportunities** are possibilities that arise from existing conditions. **Ideas** are thoughts or concepts that come from creative thinking. Ideas can come from many different sources.

### Hobbies and Interests

Many people get business ideas from their hobbies or interests. Bill had always enjoyed working with his grandfather on the farm and had helped to build and maintain many farm structures. He built a garage and added a sunroom to his own home. He also was able to make plumbing, electrical, and carpentry repairs around the house. He started doing this for others in his spare time. Soon he had so many people calling on him for these services that he decided to start a general contracting business. Identifying your hobbies and interests can help you decide what business is right for you.

## Past Experiences

Analyzing past experiences and jobs can help you come up with ideas for a business you would enjoy owning and operating. People who excel at their

How can past experiences help you succeed as an entrepreneur?

jobs have generally learned much about their profession and how to satisfy customer needs. They also see how successful marketing is conducted. Through their work, they can build a network of potential customers, suppliers, employees, and distributors. When they feel confident that they can offer a product or service to this market more effectively than their current employer, they can start a new business.

David worked as a computer network administrator for a large company. Recognizing that he could perform the same computer services for other companies, David started his own computer consulting service. He currently earns less money than he did working for a large company, but he enjoys working flexible hours and meeting new people.

## Discovery or Invention

Sometimes a business opportunity arises from a discovery or invention. Someone may invent a new tool that works better than tools that are currently available. The next step would be to research and find out if the idea can be patented, who the competition is, what the manufacturing process would be, and who the target market is.

Chandra enjoyed working in her garden, but she did not like any of the tools she had for removing weeds from around the plants. She modified one of her tools and found that it worked perfectly. After several friends tried out the tool and liked it, Chandra decided to investigate obtaining a patent for it.

## CheckPOINT

Where do new ideas for businesses come from?

_____

_____

## Tech Literacy

**SBA ON THE INTERNET**

The Internet can be a very valuable resource for entrepreneurs because it contains thousands of web pages tailored to entrepreneurs. The Small Business Administration (www.sba.gov) has a great deal of helpful information for entrepreneurs. The Small Business Planner link has information that will help you decide if entrepreneurship is right for you as well as information on how to write a business plan, start your business, and manage it. There are also links to community resources that can be helpful to a new business owner. In addition, the SBA offers free newsletters and publications.

**THINK CRITICALLY**

What type of information on the SBA website do you think would be useful if you were starting a business?

# Investigate Opportunities

People often do research to determine what is missing in a particular market—what needs exist that are not being met. By conducting this research, they hope to find the perfect business opportunity.

## Utilize Resources

The Internet and the library have resources that can help you examine different opportunities. These include books on entrepreneurship, magazines for entrepreneurs, industry trade magazines, and government publications. *County Business Patterns* is an annual series of publications providing economic profiles of counties, states, and the United States as a whole. Data include employment, payroll, and the number of establishments by industry.

This is not the only place to investigate opportunities. The Small Business Administration (SBA) is an organization that exists to help small businesses and their owners. It publishes information that may be helpful. Talking to other entrepreneurs and attending professional events and **trade shows**, which are special meetings where companies of the same or a related industry display their products, can also be beneficial.

## Compare Different Opportunities

Once you find appealing business opportunities, you need to identify which ones have the best chance for success. Now is the time to assess each business opportunity by asking yourself the following questions.

1. Is there a market in my community for this kind of business? Will people buy my product or service?

**COMMUNICATE**

Write a letter to the Small Business Administration. In your letter, indicate your interest in starting a small business. Be specific about the type of business you wish to start. Ask what specific services the SBA provides to people who wish to start this type of business.

2. How much money would it take to start this business? Will I be able to borrow that much money?

3. How many hours a week is it likely to take to run this business? Am I willing to commit that much time?

4. What are the particular risks associated with this business? What is the rate of business failure?

5. Does my background prepare me to run this kind of business? Do most people who own this kind of business have more experience than I do?

6. How much money could I make running this business? Could I make a profit after paying expenses?

## CheckPOINT

How can you find out about various business opportunities?

_____

_____

## Set Goals

For everything you do in life, you set goals. Goals help you stay on track and follow through with your plans. The best goals are SMART. Smart goals provide more direction as shown below.

| SMART GOALS | |
|---|---|
| **S**pecific | Goals should be specific and answer "What?" and "How?" |
| **M**easurable | Goals should establish ways to measure your progress |
| **A**ttainable | Goals should not be too far out of reach |
| **R**ealistic | Goals should represent things to which you are willing to commit |
| **T**imely | Goals should have a timeframe for achievement |
| **Goal** | I will learn more about starting my own business. |
| **SMART Goal** | I will learn more about starting my own catering business by obtaining information from the Small Business Administration and talking with the owners of three local catering businesses by the end of the month. |

As an entrepreneur, you will need to set many goals. Goals can be categorized as financial and nonfinancial.

## Business Math Connection

Mo Yang wants to start a mail-order business for model trains, planes, and cars. His income goal is $27,000 per year. He can buy the models for $10 and plans to sell them for $19. How many models would he need to sell to meet his income goal?

**SOLUTION**

To determine the number of models he would need to sell, Mo Yang divided his income goal by the profit for each model.

$19 − $10 = $9 profit

$27,000 ÷ $9 = 3,000 models per year

Mo Yang would have to sell 3,000 models to meet an income goal of $27,000 per year. This showed Mo that he would have to lower his income goal or find another business idea because he would probably not be able to sell that many models.

## Financial Goals

Set specific financial goals before starting a business. Financial goals can include how much money you will earn and how quickly you will pay off debts. Make sure your goals are realistic. Goals should also be measurable and easily attainable in the time allotted. If one of your goals is to make a large sum of money early on, you almost certainly will be disappointed. It usually takes time for businesses to become well established and profitable. Setting SMART financial goals will help you develop a realistic plan for earning a profit.

## Nonfinancial Goals

Most people who own their own businesses do so for more than just monetary gain. They are looking for personal satisfaction. They may serve a community need, do something they like, or enjoy the personal independence of being an entrepreneur. You will want to specify what nonfinancial goals you want to achieve by being an entrepreneur. For example, you may want to offer support to a charitable organization, either by making monetary donations or by offering your business's services. Setting and meeting nonfinancial goals can help an entrepreneur live a more satisfying and fulfilling life.

## CheckPOINT

Name some nonfinancial goals an entrepreneur may have.

_____

_____

## Think Critically

1. Think about a business opportunity that appeals to you. For this business, write your answers to the six assessment questions listed in this lesson. Is this a realistic choice for you? Why or why not?

_____

_____

_____

_____

2. In terms of annual income, what financial goals have you set for yourself for five years after you graduate? What nonfinancial goals have you set that you might be able to fulfill by becoming an entrepreneur?

_____

_____

_____

3. Your friend has set the following goal: I plan to start a lawn care business. Is this a SMART goal? Explain why or why not. What suggestions would you make for improving it?

_____

_____

_____

## Make Academic Connections

4. **Math** You live near the beach and have a passion for snorkeling. Your dream is to give snorkeling lessons. You estimate that after expenses, you can earn $10 per lesson. Each lesson will be one hour long, and you plan to offer lessons five days a week. Your income goal is $15,000 per year. How many lessons do you need to give to achieve this goal? Is this goal realistic?

_____

_____

_____

_____

5. **Social Studies** Write a personal nonfinancial goal involving your local community that you would like to achieve through entrepreneurship. Be sure the goal is SMART. Write an outline for a detailed plan you can follow to achieve this goal. Explain how it would benefit your community.

**JUMP START**

Gloria and Delia spend time on the Internet and in the local library researching ideas for their new business. As a result, they come up with several ideas. Now they have to decide what to do with these ideas. As they discuss their options, Gloria says, "You know, Delia, we can talk about these ideas, but we really need an organized system that will help us make the very best decisions for our business." "Yes," Delia responds, "You are right. I remember reading about a problem-solving model that aids the decision-making process. Let's learn more about it and see if we can adapt it for our use!" How do you think a problem-solving model can be useful in making decisions?

### GOALS

List the six steps of the problem-solving model

Describe ways to improve your problem-solving skills

### KEY TERMS

problem-solving model, p. 23

brainstorming, p. 26

## Use the Problem-Solving Process

As an entrepreneur, you will be faced with making decisions and solving problems every day. Whether or not to become an entrepreneur is a big decision. Many entrepreneurs make decisions casually or base them on intuition. As a result, their decisions are based on faulty assumptions or illogical thinking. The best entrepreneurs use formal problem-solving models to gather information and evaluate different options.

A formal **problem-solving model** helps people solve problems in a logical manner. The model consists of six steps.

## Step 1 Define the Problem

Before you can solve a problem, you need to diagnose it. Write down what the problem is. Try to quantify it also. For example, you may be trying to decide whether to start your own business or work for another company. If you accept the job offer, your income would be $30,000 a year. If you reject the job offer, you would lose that income. Quantifying the problem helps you figure out how much it is worth to you to solve it.

Dan knows what his problem is: Should he start a website design company? He took many computer courses throughout high school, and he is now attending college. He has worked in the food industry throughout high school and college. Dan enjoys working at restaurants and has gained valuable customer service and management experience. In addition, he also volunteers his web design skills on projects for his university and local community programs. He will be graduating in the next few months with a degree in Computer Science. Dan is considering starting his own website design business, but he is not sure whether that is the right choice for him.

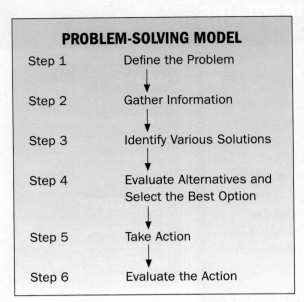

**PROBLEM-SOLVING MODEL**

Step 1 — Define the Problem

Step 2 — Gather Information

Step 3 — Identify Various Solutions

Step 4 — Evaluate Alternatives and Select the Best Option

Step 5 — Take Action

Step 6 — Evaluate the Action

## Step 2 Gather Information

Once the problem has been defined, you need to gather information that could help solve it. Relevant information may be obtained from many sources, including company records, industry data, and trade magazines. It is also a good idea to interview other people in the industry to find out what their experiences have been and to learn how they have solved similar problems.

In Dan's case, it would be helpful for him to take a closer look at himself. He should do a self-assessment to determine his strengths and weaknesses. He also needs to consider his skills, experience, and interests. Does he have the characteristics of a successful entrepreneur? He also needs to examine the advantages and disadvantages of running a website design company. He should talk to other professionals in the business and read trade magazines to gather information about running a website design business. Dan needs to explore every aspect of starting and running a website design company.

## Step 3 Identify Various Solutions

Most problems can be solved in various ways. Identify all possibilities before you settle on a particular solution. Dan comes up with several possible solutions to his problem.

1. Work as an employee in a position that utilizes his customer service skills and management experience.

2. Work as a website designer for another company to gain more experience and then start his own business in three to five years.

3. Pursue his interests in the food industry and open his own restaurant.

4. Start his own website design company upon graduation.

## Step 4 Evaluate Alternatives and Select the Best Option

The decision maker next needs to evaluate the alternatives to determine the best solution. In some cases, it may be possible to quantify the costs and benefits of each alternative. In other cases, quantifying each alternative may not be possible, and the decision maker may simply have to rank each alternative.

Dan ranks option 1 the lowest because of his strong desire to be his own boss. All of the information that Dan gathered indicates that he has a strong chance of succeeding as an entrepreneur. He ranks option 3 next to lowest. Dan has considerable experience in the food industry and enjoys that type of work, but he decides he would rather pursue his interests in website design. He ranks option 2 second because he is already confident in his level of computer knowledge and experience. After evaluating all of his alternatives, Dan decides option 4 is the best solution.

What are some ways to evaluate alternatives to help you make a decision?

## Step 5 Take Action

Once you have selected the best solution to the problem, you need to take action to implement it. Dan begins putting together a business plan and spreading the word about his new venture.

## Step 6 Evaluate the Action

The problem-solving process is not complete until you evaluate your action since even a well-thought-out solution may not work. After being in business for six months, Dan evaluates whether he is achieving his financial and nonfinancial goals. It seems that Dan made the right decision because his business is profitable and he is enjoying his work. Dan will continue to use the problem-solving model to make the most effective decisions for his new business.

## CheckPOINT

What are the six steps in the problem-solving process?

_____

_____

# Problem-Solving Skills

The problem-solving model will become a valuable tool to you throughout your career. However, there are a few other things you can do to improve your problem-solving skills.

## Communicate

Good communication is important in the problem-solving process. When trying to resolve problems and make decisions, you most likely will have to interact with others. You may have to ask questions, request information, and express your ideas and opinions. On such occasions, it is important that you communicate clearly and confidently. You must also be a good listener. You must carefully listen to information, opinions, and suggestions from others. Listening to others' input can help you make informative decisions.

## Brainstorm

**Brainstorming** is a creative problem-solving technique that involves generating a large number of fresh ideas. Brainstorming is often done in a group setting, but it is a very useful activity for an individual as well. Brainstorm by writing down as many possible solutions to your problem as you can think of. Do not be afraid to write down any idea you have. The point of brainstorming is not to judge your ideas as good or bad but to come up with as many ideas as possible. Once you have made a list of ideas, you can use the problem-solving model to determine the best alternatives.

## Learn from Mistakes

If you want to become an entrepreneur, you cannot be afraid to make mistakes. Mistakes are likely to happen, but you should view them as a learning experience. Mistakes can help you learn what to do or what not to do, which proves to be valuable in the problem-solving process.

Some of the nation's most famous entrepreneurs failed before they came up with a winning idea. Colonel Sanders of KFC fame is a good example. He held many jobs and owned a motel chain, service stations, and other restaurants that were unsuccessful. Eventually, he developed his secret recipe chicken. In 1952, at the age of 62, he began traveling by car across the country selling his chicken. By 1964, there were 600 KFC restaurants in the United States and Canada, and Colonel Sanders sold KFC for $2 million.

## CheckPOINT

How can you improve your problem-solving skills?

_____

_____

# Think Critically

1. Must the six steps in the problem-solving model be performed in the order described? Why or why not?

_____

_____

_____

_____

2. How do you think strong communication skills can improve the problem-solving process? Provide specific examples of how a business owner might use communication skills to resolve a problem.

_____

_____

_____

_____

# Make Academic Connections

3. **Math** In the *Identify Various Solutions* stage of the problem-solving model, you list a variety of possible solutions to a problem. For the four options Dan came up with on pages 24–25, assign a percentage weight to each based on Dan's reasoning. Give the decimal equivalent for each percentage. What must the decimal value of the four options total?

_____

_____

_____

4. **Problem Solving** You own a successful shop that buys, sells, and services bicycles. In January, the owner of the building you now lease tells you that she has found a buyer for the property and plans to sell it in six months. Using the six-step problem-solving model, develop a plan for how to proceed.

_____

_____

_____

_____

_____

## Chapter Summary

**1.1 All about Entrepreneurship**

A. Entrepreneurship is the process of running a business of one's own. The person who owns, operates, and takes the risks of a business venture is called an entrepreneur.

B. Factors that contribute to a new business's success include adequate capital, a product or service that meets customer needs, and the owner's education level and business experience.

**1.2 Is Entrepreneurship Right for You?**

A. Successful entrepreneurs tend to be independent, self-confident, determined, goal-oriented, and creative.

B. Entrepreneurs must have good team-building skills and be able to work well with others.

C. To determine whether entrepreneurship is right for you, you will need to assess your strengths, weaknesses, interests, and aptitudes.

**1.3 Explore Ideas and Opportunities**

A. Ideas for new businesses can come from your hobbies and interests, your past experiences, and from a discovery or invention.

B. You may investigate business opportunities through the Internet and public library, the SBA, trade shows, and other entrepreneurs.

C. Entrepreneurs should set SMART goals, which are specific, measurable, attainable, realistic, and timely.

**1.4 Problem Solving for Entrepreneurs**

A. A problem-solving model consists of six steps: define the problem, gather information, identify various solutions, evaluate alternatives and select the best option, take action, and evaluate the action.

B. There are several ways to improve problem-solving skills including communicating, brainstorming, and learning from mistakes.

## Vocabulary Builder

Choose the term that best fits the definition. Write the letter of the answer in the space provided. Some terms may not be used.

_____ 1. People who work for someone else

_____ 2. Evaluation of your strengths and weaknesses

_____ 3. Possibilities that arise from existing conditions

_____ 4. Special meetings at which companies display their products

_____ 5. People who own, operate, and take the risk of a business venture

_____ 6. Thoughts or concepts that come from creative thinking

_____ 7. The ability to learn a particular kind of job

_____ 8. The process of running a business of one's own

a. aptitude

b. brainstorming

c. employees

d. entrepreneurs

e. entrepreneurship

f. ideas

g. opportunities

h. problem-solving model

i. self-assessment

j. trade shows

# Review Concepts

9. How are entrepreneurs different from employees?

_____

_____

_____

_____

10. Why do some people go into business for themselves?

_____

_____

_____

11. Why are entrepreneurial companies important to our economy?

_____

_____

_____

12. What are the eight characteristics of a successful entrepreneur?

_____

_____

_____

_____

13. Name four different kinds of entrepreneurial businesses and describe what each produces.

_____

_____

_____

_____

14. Why is it important for a beginning entrepreneur to perform a personal assessment?

_____

_____

_____

_____

15. Why should entrepreneurs take past experiences into account when deciding to start their own business?

_____

_____

_____

_____

**16.** Why is it important to have an aptitude for the business you decide to own?

_____

_____

_____

**17.** Name some key factors that aid an entrepreneur's commitment to a business.

_____

_____

_____

_____

**18.** List the four advantages and the four disadvantages of entrepreneurship.

_____

_____

_____

_____

**19.** What resources can you use to research business opportunities?

_____

_____

_____

_____

**20.** Why should you set both financial and nonfinancial goals for yourself as an entrepreneur?

_____

_____

_____

_____

## Apply What You Learned

**21.** The categories of entrepreneurial businesses include manufacturing, wholesaling, retailing, service, agricultural, and mining and extracting. In small groups, brainstorm specific industries and companies that belong to each category of business. Try to list at least one green business for each category. Make a list of industries and companies for each type. Share your results with the class.

**22.** Think of a problem, perhaps at home or school, that you need to solve. Use the six-step problem-solving model to reach the best solution. Write a one- to two-page report describing how you completed each step.

**23.** What is the relationship between interest in and aptitude for a particular field? Can interests and aptitudes be the same? Why or why not?

_____

_____

_____

_____

**24.** Why is setting realistic financial goals important to creating a successful business?

_____

_____

_____

## Make Academic Connections

**25. History** Use the Internet to research how entrepreneurship today is different from entrepreneurship in colonial time. Write a one-page report describing what you learn.

**26. Math** Ellen Greenberg loves to make and fly kites. Ellen is planning to open a shop selling custom-made kites. She asks for your advice to help her set financial goals. Ellen estimates that after expenses, she can make a $15 profit on each kite she sells. If her annual income goal is $15,450, how many kites will she have to sell? Is this goal realistic?

_____

_____

_____

**27. Research** Find information on the life and career of a famous historical entrepreneur. Find out information such as birthplace, the type of business started, and what effect the person had on the economy and history. Is the business still operating? If so, what changes have taken place in the company since it started? Write a short report about your findings.

## Ethical Dilemma

**28.** Nancy and Gary had been best friends since elementary school. During their senior year, Nancy told Gary about an idea she had for a business in the local community. She had done some research and thought that her idea had a good chance of turning into a profitable business. After high school graduation, Nancy went away to college while Gary stayed home and went to the local community college. Since Nancy had not acted on her business idea before leaving for college, Gary decided that he would try to open a business using Nancy's idea. What do you think about Gary's actions? Is he doing the right thing?

## CHAPTER 2

# Develop a Business Plan

## Careers for Entrepreneurs

*Transportation, Distribution & Logistics*

### UPS

James E. "Jim" Casey began a messenger service delivering personal messages to homes before most people had telephones. In 1907, the U.S. Postal Service had no parcel post system, so there was also a need for luggage and packages to be delivered. By borrowing $100, Jim established the American Messenger Company. His company had strict policies: customer courtesy, reliability, round-the-clock service, and low rates. In 1919, American Messenger Company became United Parcel Service (UPS), and these principles still guide UPS today.

UPS's services have evolved over the years. It changed its focus from messenger delivery to package delivery for retail stores. Several years later, UPS began offering common carrier services, such as automatic daily pickups, which put it in direct competition with the U.S. Postal Service. Technology plays a major role in helping UPS maintain efficiency, keep prices competitive, and provide new customer services.

### Think Critically

1. What do you think contributes to the success of UPS?
2. Why has UPS changed the way it does business over the years?

# PROJECT | Get Started on Your Business Plan

## Project Objectives

- Use research sources and further planning to refine your business plan
- Begin writing components of your business plan

## Getting Started

Read the Project Process below. Make a list of any materials you will need.

- Think about the business idea you came up with in Chapter 1. If you were to start this business, where do you think it would be in one year? Five years? Ten years?
- Make a list of places and people you think you could consult for assistance in developing your business idea.

Photodisc/Getty Images

## Project Process

**2.1** Explain why there is a market/need for your product or service. Survey five or more people to learn how many show interest in it? Prepare a one-page report describing your product or service and what makes it unique.

**2.2** List your short-, medium-, and long-term goals. What steps do you need to take to achieve each of these goals? Begin the financial section of your business plan by writing a report that identifies the risks your business faces. For each risk, explain how you will overcome the problem.

**2.3** Contact the Small Business Administration, a Small Business Development Center, or a SCORE volunteer to get information for your type of business. Write about the industry in which you will be competing.

## Chapter Review

**Project Wrap-up** Key the information that you have prepared in this project in an attractive format. This will be the beginning of your business plan.

© Sean De Burca, 2009/ Used under license from Shutterstock.com

**GOALS**

Explain the purpose of writing a good business plan

Describe the importance of a business plan

**KEY TERM**

business plan, p. 34

 **JUMP START**

Nora Ellis and Samantha Richards are qualified childcare workers who have worked together at a day-care center for many years. The center frequently turned away children because it did not have the room or the staff to take care of more toddlers. Nora and Samantha realized they could make a profit running their own day-care center and decided to open a center of their own. Everyone they talked to about their idea said it sounded good and wanted to see their business plan. They realized the need for a good business plan to help ensure their business would succeed. Why do you think a business plan is important for someone starting a business?

Photodisc/Getty Images

## Purpose of a Business Plan

Once you have worked out the details of your business, you need to put everything down on paper. Writing out these details will help you visualize all the aspects of your business. It will also help you convince banks and other people to invest in your business idea. A **business plan** is a written document that describes all the steps necessary to open and operate a successful business. Writing a business plan is one of the most difficult and important things you will do as an entrepreneur. Writing a solid business plan is critical because the plan can make or break your business.

The business plan

• Describes what your business will produce, how you will produce it, and who will buy your product or service

- Explains who will run your business and who will supply it with goods
- States how your business will win over customers from competitors and what your business will do to keep customers
- Provides detailed financial information that shows how your business will succeed in earning a profit

The business plan serves three important purposes.

1. **A business plan explains the idea behind your business and spells out how your product or service will be produced or sold.** To convince investors that your business idea is solid, you will need a completely new product or service or one that is better or less expensive than products or services that already exist. You will need to identify who your target customer is and show how your company will be able to obtain and keep customers.

2. **A business plan sets specific objectives and describes how your business expects to achieve them.** A good business plan includes sales projections for the short term (the first year), the medium term (two to five years after startup), and the long term (five years in the future). It describes what products and services will be introduced over the next five years and sets forth future business plans, such as expansion of the business.

3. **A business plan describes the backgrounds and experience of the people who will be running the business.** Banks and other lenders make financing decisions based on how well they think a company can meet its objectives. If you provide information on the background and experience of the people who will be running your company, the bank or investor will be more likely to invest money in your business.

Creatas/Jupiter Images

Why is a business plan important to the success of the business?

## Importance of a Business Plan

Every new business must have a business plan. When comparing businesses that succeed to those that fail, there is often one important difference—the business plan. Business owners that develop and follow a business plan are more likely to succeed than business owners who do not have a business plan. The business plan is important for several reasons.

1. **A business plan makes you think about all aspects of your business.** Stan Meyer began a graphic design business from his home. He spent many hours visualizing the business and thought he was ready to start it until he sat down to write his business plan. He had not made sales and profit projections. He had also not thought about the possibility of needing to hire staff if the business grew too large for him to handle alone. Drafting a business plan helped Stan gain even more confidence in his business idea. It showed him that building a successful business based on his concept would be possible. Working on his business plan also helped Stan think through business strategies, recognize limits, and identify problems he might encounter.

2. **A business plan may help you secure financing for your business.** Lenders require a business plan before they will consider financing a business. Without a business plan you will not be able to obtain a business loan. Lenders will review the financial section of the business plan, which will state how much money is needed to operate the business and how the money will be used. Lenders will also be interested in the financial projections showing estimated revenue, expenses, and profit.

3. **A business plan helps you communicate your ideas to others.** By the time you write your business plan, you will have given much thought to the business that you want to establish. You will also believe that your business will succeed. If you communicate your ideas well on paper, you will convince the reader that your business will succeed. This can help you get a loan from a bank. It also may convince suppliers to extend credit to your business.

When making decisions about loans, loan officers look at industry information, location, marketing plans, and your qualifications and experience. They want to be sure that you and your business are good risks and that you will be able to repay the money they loan you. The amount of the monthly payment will be calculated, and the bank will determine if you can meet the repayment plan. If Nora and Samantha need a bank loan of $55,000 and the bank offers them a five-year loan at an interest rate of 8 percent per year, what is their monthly payment?

**SOLUTION**

To calculate interest, use the following formula.

Interest = Principal × Rate × Time
Interest = $55,000 × 0.08 × 5 = $22,000

To calculate the monthly payment, use the following formula.

(Principal + Interest) ÷ Total Number of Payments = Monthly Payment
($55,000 + $22,000) ÷ 60 months          = $1,283.33

4. **A business plan can serve as a tool for managing your business.** Once your business is up and running, you can use the business plan in your decision making. It acts as a guide for business operations. It can also be used to track whether your business is developing according to plan.

Adam Rothwell regularly uses his business plan to help manage his company, Suburban Pools. Adam's plan laid out his vision of how the company would grow over time. By following the strategies he described in his plan, he has increased sales by offering new products and by targeting a larger area.

©maga, 2009/ Used under license from Shutterstock.com

How can a business plan be used to manage a business?

## CheckPOINT

Why is a business plan important to an entrepreneur?

_____

_____

## Think Critically

1. Why do you think the quality of the business plan is so critical to an entrepreneur's success?

_____

_____

_____

2. Melinda Rosati wants to purchase her uncle's barbershop. Because it is an ongoing business, Melinda doesn't think she needs to write a business plan. Do you agree or disagree with Melinda's opinion? Why or why not?

_____

_____

_____

3. Putting your business plan in writing helps you communicate your ideas to others. Do you think discussing your business plan out loud in a meeting can also help you get your ideas across? Why or why not?

_____

_____

_____

## Make Academic Connections

4. **Problem Solving** André Kitaevich uses the business plan he wrote to help him run the day-to-day operations in his jewelry store. On what specific issues might André consult his plan?

_____

_____

5. **Communication** You are starting a business in the home healthcare field. Write a paragraph explaining the idea behind the business. Be sure to spell out how you plan to market its services.

6. **Math** If Nora and Samantha need a bank loan of $75,000 and the bank offers them a five-year loan at an interest rate of 9 percent per year, what is their monthly payment?

_____

_____

_____

### JUMP START

As they began working on their business plan, Nora and Samantha realized that it was not going to be an easy task. There was a great deal of necessary information that needed to go in the plan. They were going to have to do a lot of research and make plans for the future of their business. The business plan needed to present a clear picture of their idea so that anyone who read it would understand their plans and intentions. What types of things do you think Nora and Samantha should include in their business plan?

## Basic Elements of a Business Plan

Every new business should have a business plan, but not all business plans are alike. The content of a business plan for a small, home-based, sole-owner business will differ from a business plan for a large corporation with offices in many cities. But regardless of the business, all business plans serve the same basic purposes. They should also contain the same three basic components—introductory elements, the main body, and the appendix.

The main body of the business plan will contain the bulk of the information about the business idea. It provides details on how the business will succeed. A lot of time and effort will go into writing the main body of the plan, and it should be compiled first. Then, details from the main body will be used to compile the other components in the business plan.

The main body of the business plan will cover many areas. It should be organized into five sections.

1. Introduction
2. Marketing
3. Financial Management
4. Operations
5. Concluding Statement

Nora Ellis and Samantha Richards are qualified childcare providers who have worked together at a day-care center for many years. Because of the high demand for quality day-care services, Nora and Samantha know they are well positioned to meet this need. They decide to create a business plan for opening their own center.

## Introduction

The introduction section of a business plan contains many important details about the proposed business idea. The following information should be included in the introduction section.

- A detailed description of the business and its goals
- The ownership of the business and the legal structure
- The skills and experience you bring to the business
- The advantages you and your business have over your competitors

### Detailed Description

Something inspired the idea for your business. Describing how you came up with your idea can help lenders, investors, and others understand what your business is about. Your business plan should also outline your short-term (three months to one year), medium-term (two to five years), and long-term (more than five years) goals. This section describes your vision for the company's future. Stating goals will help provide you with direction and focus for your business activities.

Nora and Samantha know their short- and medium-term goals. In the first year of business, they want to get financing to lease or buy a facility, equip the facility, and staff it. By their third year of business, they want to invest in more equipment and expand their facility. They have not yet thought about their long-term objectives. Writing a business plan will force them to think about future plans.

Why should you include goals in your business plan?

©Stephen Coburn, 2009/ Used under license from Shutterstock.com

**Ownership and Legal Structure** In your business, you should have a section detailing your form of ownership. Will it be a sole proprietorship (one owner), a partnership (two or more owners), or a corporation (many owners that hold shares of stock in the business)? Provide information relevant to your form of business, such as who your partners are or how many shareholders you have. This section of the business plan is important because each legal form of business has an effect on how the business works and makes profits.

**Skills and Experience** A written summary of your experience is an essential part of your business plan. This summary should emphasize all experience you have that relates to the business, including paid work experience, volunteer experience, and any hobbies you have that relate to your proposed business. The skills and experience of any managers or professional employees who will be hired will also be relevant.

Nora and Samantha have Master's degrees in early childhood education. Together, they have more than 35 years of experience in day care, including 15 years in management. To show that they are well qualified to run a day-care center, they include copies of their resumes and letters of reference from satisfied parents.

**Competitive Advantages** You should list your company's advantages over the competition. These advantages may include the following.

- Performance
- Quality
- Reliability
- Distribution
- Price
- Promotion
- Public image or reputation

## Tech Literacy

### PREPARING THE BUSINESS PLAN

There are many software programs available for entrepreneurs to use when preparing a business plan. A recent Internet search showed more than 345,000 matches for "business plan software." Many entrepreneurs use these programs because they provide an easy-to-use template. By plugging your specific information into the template, you get a professional-looking finished report. If you decide to use a software program to create your business plan, be sure it includes all of the essential elements. It is a good idea to evaluate several different programs before deciding which one to use. Your choice should best match the information you want to include and your desired style. And, of course, it should be one that you can use without difficulty.

### THINK CRITICALLY

What are some of the advantages and disadvantages of using business plan software?

## Marketing

The marketing section of your business plan should describe the products and/or services you will offer, the market, the industry, and your location. Developing a marketing plan will be examined in more detail in Chapter 4.

**Products and Services** Describe the products or services and explain how they differ from those already on the market. Highlight any unique features of your products or services, and explain the benefits customers will receive by purchasing from your company.

**Market** You will explain who your prospective customers are, how large the market is for your product or service, and how you plan to enter that market. You should also explain how you plan to deal with competition.

Writing this section of the business plan was easy for Nora and Samantha because they had a clear idea of what they wanted to do. Their prospective customers are the parents of the 1,000 to 1,500 children between the ages of two and five who live in their area. Nora and Samantha determine that 90 percent of the families would be able to afford their center. They will advertise in local newspapers and send out fliers to families in their target market.

**Industry** You should describe the industry in which you will operate. To find this information, you will need to conduct research. Things you should include in this section are

- External factors affecting your business, such as high competition or a lack of certain suppliers
- Growth potential of the industry, including growth forecasts
- Economic trends of the industry
- Technology trends that may affect the industry

When providing information on the industry in which they will operate, Nora and Samantha include population data for their area. This information shows that demand for their service could grow over time.

Why would population data be useful in the development of the marketing plan?

**Location**  Describe the location of your business. Lenders want to know exactly where your business will be because the location is often a critical factor in its success.

Nora and Samantha describe their plan to start the business in a prime location, in the heart of a suburb where most families have young children and both parents work outside the home.

**TEAMWORK**

In small groups, brainstorm reasons why it is important to include each of the elements of a business plan.

## Financial Management

The financial section of your business plan will help determine your financial needs. It forces you to look at financial risks and the costs and expenses of running your business. It consists of three elements.

1. **Identification of Risks**  Prospective lenders and investors will want to know what risks your business faces and how you plan to deal with them. Do not be afraid to list potential problems. Lenders know that every business faces risks. They will be reassured to see that you have clearly thought through the potential problems and have a plan for dealing with them. Risks typically faced by new businesses include competitors cutting prices, costs exceeding projections, and demand for your product or service declining.

2. **Financial Statements**  A new business must include projected financial statements in its business plan. An existing business must include current as well as projected statements. A financial statement based on projected revenues and expenses is called a **pro forma financial statement**.

©Stephen Aaron Rees, 2009/ Used under license from Shutterstock.com

Why is it important to prepare projected financial statements for a new business?

3. **Funding Request and Return on Investment**  You must indicate how much you need to borrow and how you plan to use the money. You should give investors an idea of how much money they could expect to earn on their investment in your business. You should state how much money you are personally investing and provide a personal financial statement.

Nora and Samantha have included pro forma financial statements for their business, which show how much money and profit they expect to earn. They require $140,000 to start their business. Together they are contributing $85,000 of their own money. This means they need a bank to loan them $55,000. They include this information in their plan as well.

## Operations

The operation of your company is critical to its success. In this section of your business plan, you should explain how the business will be managed on a day-to-day basis and discuss hiring and personnel procedures. You should also include information on insurance and lease or rental

Why should you consider your hiring needs when preparing a business plan?

agreements. Describe the equipment that will be necessary for production of your products or services and how the products or services will be produced and delivered.

As part of the operations section of their business plan, Nora and Samantha describe hiring plans to ensure their day-care center is well staffed. They also devote a section to health and safety and outline plans for dealing with emergencies.

## Concluding Statement

In this section, you should summarize the goals and objectives you have for your business. You should also emphasize your commitment to the success of the business.

---

## CheckPOINT

Why should the business plan include information about the business owner's skills and experience?

_____

_____

---

## Complete the Business Plan

After you have completed the main body of your business plan, you will need to focus your efforts on the other components—the introductory elements and the appendix. Then you must pull all the components together into a well-organized, attractive document.

## Introductory Elements

Every business plan should begin with a cover letter, a title page, a table of contents, a statement of purpose, and an executive summary. These elements help set the tone for the body of your business plan.

**Cover Letter** A letter that introduces and explains an accompanying document or set of documents is called a **cover letter**. The cover letter for your business plan should include your name, the name of your business, and your address and telephone number. It should briefly describe your business and its potential for success. It also needs to tell the reader how much capital you need. Nora and Samantha prepare the cover letter shown below.

THE MT. WASHINGTON

C E N T E R

5813 NORTH AVENUE, BALTIMORE, MARYLAND 21205

(410) 555-4445

April 11, 20—

Ms. Jane Stewart
Vice President
First National Bank
East 35th Street
Baltimore, Maryland 21212

Dear Ms. Stewart:

Enclosed please find a copy of the business plan for the Mt. Washington Chidren's Center, a proposed new day-care center in northwest Baltimore that will serve approximately 50 young children. We believe that the acute shortage of high-quality day care in this part of the city will allow us to generate significant revenues for the center and that we will be earning a profit within a year of opening.

To establish the kind of center we envision, we plan to put up $85,000 of our own capital. We will need additional financing of $55,000. As you will note from our pro forma financial statements, we plan to repay the loan within five years.

Please let us know if there is any additional information you would like to receive. We look forward to hearing from you.

Sincerely yours,

*Nora Ellis*
Nora Ellis

*Samantha Richards*
Samantha Richards

Enclosure

**Title Page** Your business plan should have a title page that indicates the name of your company, the current date, the owner of the company, the title of the owner, and the address and phone number of the company.

**Table of Contents** A table of contents is a listing of the material included in a publication. It shows the reader what each page covers. It is similar to a table of contents in a textbook. It is important that your table of contents is accurate, so make sure the sections are listed in the proper order and the given page numbers are correct.

**Statement of Purpose** A brief explanation of why you are asking for a loan and what you plan to do with the money is called a **statement of purpose**. It should be no more than one or two paragraphs. Nora and Samantha write the statement of purpose shown here.

---

STATEMENT OF PURPOSE

The Mt. Washington Children's Center will operate as a private day-care center serving approximately 50 children in northwest Baltimore. The Center will offer excellent supervision in a clean, safe, and intellectually stimulating environment.

The project is requesting $55,000 in financing. This money will be used to
- rent and remodel 4,000 square feet of indoor space
- prepare 18,000 square feet of outdoor space for use as a playground
- purchase equipment such as swings, jungle gyms, sandboxes, and supplies
- pay salaries of eight employees until sufficient cash flow is generated to allow operating expenses to be covered

---

**Executive Summary** Before getting into the detail of the main body of the business plan, readers will want to read an executive summary. An **executive summary** is a short restatement of the report. It should capture the interest of its readers and make them want to read more. If the executive summary is unconvincing, a lender may decide not to read your entire business plan. This makes a strong executive summary critical to the success of your business.

The executive summary should be no longer than one or two pages, and it should be written in a clear, simple style. Your executive summary should do all of the following.

- Describe your business concept and communicate what is unique about your idea

- Include your projections for sales, costs, and profits

- Identify your needs (inventory, land, building, equipment, etc.)

- State the amount you are interested in borrowing

Although the executive summary appears before the body of the business plan, it should be written after the business plan has been completed. To write the executive summary, go through

Why is the executive summary one of the most important elements of a business plan?

## EXECUTIVE SUMMARY

The Mt. Washington Children's Center (MWCC) will be established as a partnership in Baltimore, Maryland. It will be owned and operated by Nora Ellis and Samantha Richards, highly respected childcare professionals with more than 35 years of experience in the field. Three experienced teachers and three teacher aides will supervise approximately 50 boys and girls between the ages of 2 and 5. In addition, a receptionist/bookkeeper and a cleaning/maintenance person will be hired.

MWCC is being established in response to the shortage of high-quality childcare in northwest Baltimore. Only two small day-care centers now serve a population of 45,000 upper-middle-class professionals. In 75 percent of these households, both parents work outside the home. The accessible location of the Center will make it an extremely attractive day-care option for parents in the area. When completed, the facility, which will include four large outdoor play structures and eight personal computers, will represent state-of-the-art day care. Its staff will comprise the finest day-care professionals in Baltimore, led by a management team that is recognized throughout the region.

Market research indicates that the MWCC could expect to fill 90 to 100 percent of its student positions immediately upon opening and that the Center would be profitable as early as the third year of operation. Expansion could begin in the third year. To finance the startup of the company, its owners are seeking $55,000 in financing, which they would expect to repay within five years.

the business plan and find the most important and persuasive points you have made. Then draft an outline of an executive summary based on these points.

Once you have created a draft of your executive summary, ask people who do and do not understand your business to read the summary. If readers do not come away with a clear sense of what you plan to do and why you will succeed in doing it, your executive summary needs more work. Nora and Samantha's executive summary is shown above.

## Appendix

The appendix to the business plan includes supporting documents that provide additional information and back up statements made in the body of the report. To help you determine what supporting documents to include, you should ask yourself what you would want to know about a business before you would lend it money. Documents that might be included in the appendix are shown in the following list.

- Tax returns of the business owner for the past three years
- Personal financial statement of the owner
- Copy of proposed lease or purchase agreement for the building space
- Copy of business licenses and other legal documents
- Copy of resume of the owner
- Letters of recommendation
- Copies of letters of intent from suppliers
- Copies of any large sales contracts you have already negotiated

## Put It All Together

Your business plan is your best opportunity to let other people know what you want to do with your company. It gives you the chance to convince them that your idea is sound and that you have the talent and resources to make your idea a successful business venture. To make the best of this opportunity, you will want to create an attractive document that is neat, well organized, and inviting to read. Handwritten business plans are not acceptable. All business plans must be word processed and printed on standard-sized

How can you create an attractive business plan?

white paper. In addition, your business plan should follow a standard format containing the introductory elements, the main body, and the appendix.

## CheckPOINT

Why should you include supporting documents in your business plan?

_____

_____

_____

# Think Critically

1. Why is it possible to write an executive summary only after you have written the main body of your business plan? Why might the executive summary be more important than the body of the plan?

_____

_____

_____

2. Why do you think it is important to include management and staffing issues in the operations section of your business plan?

_____

_____

_____

3. A group of investors is planning to open a new amusement park. What supporting documents will need to be included in their business plan?

_____

_____

_____

_____

# Make Academic Connections

4. **Math** You plan to start a corporation. You have $67,500 in savings, but you need $165,000 total to begin your business. How much money will you need from investors? What will be your percentage of ownership? If you have four outside investors, how much will each investor need to invest equally? What percentage will each investor own?

_____

_____

_____

5. **Communication** An entrepreneur's resume is an important supporting document for a business plan. Research resume formats and choose one that you think would be suitable for you. Prepare a resume that identifies your experience and qualifications for running a business.

6. **Research** Using the Internet, find the names of at least three business plan software programs. Make a list of the features of each program and its cost. Evaluate the programs and decide which one you would select if you wanted to use a software program to prepare a business plan.

**JUMP START**

As Nora and Samantha continued working on their business plan, they found themselves spending a lot of time at the local library and on the Internet. There was so much that they needed to find out about the childcare business. They were also visiting other day-care centers in the area and interviewing the owners. They wanted to make certain their business plan covered all the important aspects of their business. Because their business plan would be used to get a business loan, Nora and Samantha wanted to avoid making any mistakes. What other resources might be helpful in preparing their business plan? How can they avoid making any mistakes?

©Stephen Coburn, 2009/ Used under license from Shutterstock.com

## Research the Business Plan

Your business plan needs to convince readers that you have come up with a practical business idea. To do this, you must include information and data from objective sources to show that your idea is founded on solid evidence.

Researching and writing a business plan takes time. Most entrepreneurs spend 50 to 100 hours developing their business plans. The process requires patience, research, thought, and a great deal of writing and editing.

Pulling together the information you will need to write your business plan involves researching all aspects of your business, from leasing space, to what you will charge for your product or service, to dealing with competitors. Researching all the parts of your business will teach you a great deal about running a business and may provide you with specific ideas for starting a company. There are many sources available to aid in the research process.

## Community, Government, and Professional Resources

When writing a business plan, you will likely need to seek out advice from others. People from many organizations can help you with your business plan. Available resources include the SBA, the SBDC, SCORE, your local chamber of commerce, trade associations, and professional business consultants.

**The SBA** The U.S. **Small Business Administration (SBA)** is an independent agency of the federal government that was created to help Americans start, build, and grow businesses. The SBA also provides aid, counsel, and assistance to protect the interests of small business concerns, to preserve free competitive enterprise, and to maintain and strengthen the overall economy of our nation.

**The SBDC** The Office of **Small Business Development Centers (SBDC)** provides management assistance to current and prospective small business owners. Counselors from the SBDC provide free one-on-one assistance in developing a business plan. They also provide inexpensive workshops on topics that may help you develop your plan. SBDCs have many resources in one place to assist individuals and small businesses. SBDCs were formed as a cooperative effort of the private sector, the educational community, and federal, state, and local governments. They enhance economic development by providing small businesses with training and technical assistance. Assistance from an SBDC is available to anyone who cannot afford the services of a private consultant and who is interested in beginning a small business for the first time or improving or expanding an existing small business.

**SCORE** Another source of valuable assistance is SCORE. The **Service Corps of Retired Executives (SCORE)** is made up of more than 10,500 retired executives who volunteer their time to provide entrepreneurs with real-world advice and know-how. They provide free confidential advice that could be helpful to you as you prepare your business plan. You can set up a meeting with a SCORE volunteer, or you can work with a SCORE volunteer over the Internet. SCORE also offers workshops, which are a valuable way to learn more about doing business and to network with other business professionals who can help you succeed. The topics of the workshops focus on important small business issues, ranging from business planning and marketing to web-based retailing. The SCORE counselors represent every business area. Some have worked as executives at Fortune 500 companies while others were small business owners themselves. SCORE can provide assistance for you for just a few sessions or a number of years, based on your needs.

**Chamber of Commerce** In many communities, the local Chamber of Commerce offers assistance and information to entrepreneurs. It can provide information on local resources, zoning, and licensing as well as trends affecting local businesses.

**DID YOU KNOW ?**

Since 1964, SCORE has provided online and face-to-face small business consulting to over 6.7 million entrepreneurs.

**Trade Associations** Organizations made up of professionals in a specific industry are called **trade associations**. They exist to provide information, education, and networking opportunities for individuals in their industry. These associations can be valuable sources of information to entrepreneurs.

**Professional Consultants** Some entrepreneurs hire experts to help them. Professional business consultants can be found in directories available in your library or on the Internet.

**Financial Institutions** Many entrepreneurs are not familiar with the financial aspect of starting and running a business. When writing the financial section of your business plan, it may be beneficial to talk with a banker and an accountant. They can help answer your questions about loans and financial statements.

## Print Resources

Information for your business plan can come from many print sources. Your public library will have many books on entrepreneurship that may provide you with valuable information on running your own business. In addition, books on marketing, financing, hiring and managing a staff, purchasing a business, and operating a franchise can be helpful. The library will also have books devoted specifically to writing a business plan that include sample business plans.

©matka_Wariatka, 2009/ Used under license from Shutterstock.com

What kind of print resources might be helpful when writing a business plan?

Magazines may also prove helpful—especially magazines devoted to small business ownership and to the industry in which you will be competing. Ask your librarian to help you find magazines that contain information that may be relevant to your business plan.

Government documents, including publications issued by the Small Business Administration and other federal agencies, may provide you with useful information. The SBA district office nearest you will have many publications that can help you complete your business plan.

## Online Resources

Much of the information you can find in print resources is also available on the Internet. The SBA, SBDC, and SCORE websites contain much of the same information that is provided in print. Many magazine articles that deal with entrepreneurial topics can be found online. In addition, there are many sites specifically for entrepreneurs and small businesses that may give you detailed information. Internet search engines can help you locate resources.

Nora and Samantha, who are starting their own day-care business, began research for their business plan by reading books from the library. They also read information on day-care facilities that they received from the Small Business Administration. They found many samples of business plans on the Internet that they were able to adapt to meet their needs. Once they had an outline prepared for their business plan, they met with a counselor from their local Small Business Development Center to get feedback and advice for improving their business plan. The number of hours spent on research helped Nora and Samantha prepare an effective business plan.

## CheckPOINT

What are some of the resources that are available to help you develop your business plan?

_____

_____

_____

## Mistakes in Business Planning

Many entrepreneurs will not take the necessary time to carefully plan their business and prepare their business plan. This can contribute to difficulties in getting their business started as well as business failure.

To create an effective business plan, avoid making the following common mistakes.

1. **Unrealistic Financial Projections**   Many investors will go straight to the financial section of the business plan, so it is very important for the projections in this section to be realistic. Projections should be based on solid evidence for the potential growth of the company.

2. **An Undefined Target Market**   You must clearly define your market and give a clear picture of your potential customers. Clearly explain why these customers will buy your product. Be realistic about your market and do not assume that everyone will want to buy your product or service.

3. **Poor Research**   Many potential business owners are anxious to get their business operating and do not spend the time necessary to do good research. Use up-to-date research information and verify the facts and figures in your business plan.

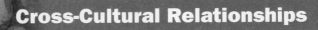

### INTERNATIONAL MARKETS

If a business plans to export products or services, it must carefully plan strategies to ensure it succeeds. Factors to consider during the planning process include the following.

- Identify the most profitable international markets. Do not select too many markets initially. Test one market and then expand as you gain more experience doing business globally.
- Determine whether you need to modify your product or service. Other countries will have different customs and specific consumer preferences. For example, Pizza Hut offers squid as a pizza topping in Japan.
- Understand international regulations and licenses that apply to your product.
- Determine the distribution method for your product or service. Consider the steps to take to export from the United States.
- Create a promotional strategy for your product or service. Consider whether you will travel to the international markets to promote your product or service or hire someone who is familiar with the markets you are targeting.

### Think Critically

What types of things should you consider when preparing to do business internationally?

4. **Ignored Competition**   Do not overlook the competition and do not focus only on what the competition has done wrong. Investors want to see who your competition is and how you plan to compete in the market. Outline how you will differentiate yourself from the competition.

5. **Inconsistencies in the Business Plan**   It is important to review your final business plan and be sure that your plan is well written and formatted in an attractive style. Be sure that information provided is consistent from section to section. It is a good idea to have an objective person review your final business plan before you show it to investors.

## CheckPOINT

List some common mistakes that are made in business planning.

_____

_____

# Think Critically

1. Why do you think it would be helpful to speak with people from community, government, or professional organizations before you write your business plan? Can you think of other people besides those mentioned in the chapter who might be good resources?

_____

_____

_____

2. Some elements of the business plan require outside source information. If your business manufactures clothing, what specific sources might you need to consult?

_____

_____

_____

3. Why is it important for financial projections to be as realistic and accurate as possible when writing your business plan?

_____

_____

4. Why is it important to carefully research global markets before doing business internationally?

_____

_____

# Make Academic Connections

5. **Language Arts** Locate an article about business plans in the library or on the Internet. Write two paragraphs summarizing the main points of the article.

6. **Math** If you intend to borrow 20 percent of the $174,500 you need to start a business, how much of your own funds are you investing?

_____

_____

7. **Research** Obtain a copy of a business plan. Possible sources include the Internet, SBA, SBDC, or SCORE. Review the business plan and list the features that you think are effective. Explain why. Then list the features that you think need improvement. Explain why. Describe any changes you would make to the business plan.

## Chapter Summary

**2.1 Why a Business Plan Is Important**

A. A business plan is a written document that describes what your business will produce, how you will produce it, and who will buy it. It also describes the backgrounds of the people running the business.

B. Writing a business plan makes you think about all aspects of your business, helps you secure financing, helps you communicate your ideas to others, and can serve as a tool for managing your business.

**2.2 What Goes into a Business Plan?**

A. The main body of the business plan should include the following sections: Introduction, Marketing, Financial Management, Operations, and Concluding Statement.

B. To complete the business plan, you need to prepare introductory elements consisting of the cover letter, title page, table of contents, statement of purpose, and executive summary. The executive summary should not be written until the main body of the plan is complete. An appendix will include supporting documents.

**2.3 How to Create an Effective Business Plan**

A. People from many organizations—including the SBA, SBDC, SCORE, your local chamber of commerce, trade associations, business consultants, and financial institutions—can help you with your business plan. Print resources are available at the library and government agencies. Information is also available on the Internet.

B. Common mistakes made in business planning include unrealistic financial projections, an undefined target market, poor research, ignored competition, and inconsistencies in the business plan.

## Vocabulary Builder

Choose the term that best fits the definition. Write the letter of the answer in the space provided. Some terms may not be used.

_____ 1. A document describing the steps for opening and operating a business

_____ 2. A financial statement based on projected revenues and expenses

_____ 3. A letter introducing an accompanying document or set of documents

_____ 4. A short restatement of a report

_____ 5. A brief explanation of why you are asking for a loan and how you will use the money

_____ 6. An agency of the federal government that helps Americans start, build, and grow businesses

_____ 7. Organizations made up of professionals in a specific industry

_____ 8. Retired executives who provide entrepreneurs with advice

a. business plan

b. cover letter

c. executive summary

d. pro forma financial statement

e. Service Corps of Retired Executives (SCORE)

f. Small Business Administration (SBA)

g. Small Business Development Centers (SBDC)

h. statement of purpose

i. trade associations

## Review Concepts

Point Your
**Browser**
www.cengage.com/
school/business/21biz

9. For whom is a business plan written?

_____

_____

_____

10. Why is writing a business plan so important?

_____

_____

_____

_____

11. What three purposes does a business plan fulfill?

_____

_____

_____

_____

12. How can a business plan help you run your business?

_____

_____

_____

_____

13. Why should entrepreneurs identify short-, medium-, and long-term goals?

_____

_____

_____

_____

14. Where can you find industry data you may need for your business plan?

_____

_____

_____

_____

15. Why is it important to identify the risks you face?

_____

_____

_____

_____

16. What factors make an appendix to your business plan necessary?

_____

_____

_____

17. Why do you need to do research to write a business plan?

_____

_____

18. Why should a business plan be word processed and follow a standard format?

_____

_____

19. What should the cover letter of your business plan do?

_____

_____

_____

## Apply What You Learned

20. You want to open a retail auto parts store. Your business plan will be aimed at lenders and suppliers. Which elements of the business plan will be of most interest to them? Which elements will require extensive research? What sources do you think will be most helpful?

_____

_____

_____

_____

21. You are planning to open a skateboarding store. What research do you need to conduct in order to write your business plan? What sources will you consult to obtain this information? To whom will your business plan be directed?

_____

_____

_____

_____

22. Writing a business plan is a fundamental part of starting your own company. Do you think entrepreneurs ever need to update their business plans? Why or why not?

_____

_____

_____

23. How do you think a business plan for a home-based business differs from that of a large corporation? How would a business plan for a manufacturing business differ from that of a service business?

_____

_____

_____

_____

24. There is a great deal of free advice available on starting and running a small business. Why do you think the government provides so much information and free help to entrepreneurs?

_____

_____

_____

## Make Academic Connections

25. **Math** You are seeking a $500,000 interest-free loan to purchase and run a 75-unit self-storage rental facility. The loan has a 10-year term. Your business plan indicates that each unit will be rented for $100 per month. Are you a good risk? What aspects besides your pro forma financial statements will the loan officer consider?

_____

_____

_____

_____

26. **Research** Contact a local insurance agent and obtain information about property insurance. You may also find information in magazines or on the Internet. Write a business plan section devoted to insurance issues.

27. **Communication** Think about a business you would like to start. Assume you will need a startup loan. With a partner, role-play a meeting between you and a loan officer.

## Ethical Dilemma

28. You have a great idea for a business you want to start. You know you need a business plan to help you secure a loan to start the business, but because you are going to school full time and are working nights and weekends, you do not have time to prepare one. While searching the Internet, you find a business plan for a company that is similar to the one you want to start. It would save you time if you copied this plan, changed the business name, and added your personal information. What would you do? What problems might this cause?

## CHAPTER 3

# Select a Type of Ownership

**3.1** Run an Existing Business

**3.2** Own a Franchise or Start a Business

**3.3** Choose the Legal Form of Your Business

## Careers for Entrepreneurs

### GOOGLE

What would the Internet be like if there was no Google? Sergey Brin and Larry Page "set out to organize the world's information and make it universally accessible and useful!" Brin and Page developed a new approach to online searching while they were students at Stanford University. Using that approach, they launched Google in September of 1998 as a privately held company. Today, Google is one of the world's best-known brands. Most people have learned about Google by word of mouth from satisfied users.

Google generates revenue by selling advertising space. Ads are displayed on search results pages that are relevant to the content on the page. Google tracks customer traffic to measure the cost-effectiveness of the online advertising.

Today, Brin and Page share a net worth of $18.5 billion. Google handles nearly 3 billion search inquiries daily. That's not bad for a data center that started in a dorm room!

### Think Critically

1. What would be the advantages to Brin and Page if they sold stock in their company?
2. What would be the disadvantages to Brin and Page if their company stock was publicly traded?

## Project Objectives

- Consider the purchase of existing businesses
- Research franchise opportunities
- Learn more about partnerships and S corporations

©Peter Gudella, 2009/ Used under license from Shutterstock.com

## Getting Started

Read the Project Process below. Make a list of any materials you will need.

- Using the business opportunity you decided upon in Chapter 1, make a list of the businesses that would compete with you within a 10-mile radius of where you are thinking of locating your business.
- If there are no businesses of a similar nature to yours, write a statement telling why your business is unique and why there is no competition for it.

## Project Process

**3.1** You are considering developing your business idea by purchasing an existing business. Using the list you developed in Getting Started, write down the reasons you would or would not consider buying each company.

**3.2** Find franchise opportunities available in your business field. Gather information such as franchise fees, royalties, projected earnings, and operating costs. If you start your own business, assume you will franchise it. Write an advertisement offering to sell franchises to prospective owners.

**3.3** You have a friend who is interested in being your business partner. Write the partnership agreement for the two of you. In addition, list the advantages and disadvantages of becoming an S corporation.

## Chapter Review

**Project Wrap-up** Decide whether you will purchase an existing business or a franchise or start a new business. Prepare a report explaining your choice.

©Monkey Business Images, 2009/Used under license from Shutterstock.com

**JUMP START**

On graduation day from the Culinary Arts Institute, Abbie and Kaito realized that they had decisions to make if their dream of opening their own bakery was going to happen. Kaito saw an ad about a bakery for sale owned by the Holcombe family. Abbie was familiar with the bakery. She remembered that the last time she visited the bakery, no one was waiting on the customers, and people were becoming upset. What are some other problems that an existing business might have?

YOUR LOCAL FAMILY BAKERS

737

Photodisc/Getty Images

## Choose an Existing Business

Before making the decision to purchase an existing business, an entrepreneur must determine why the business is for sale. Business owners sell their businesses for a variety of reasons. These can include insufficient sales or profits, worry about new competition, fear of new economic conditions, retirement, a dispute between partners, the death or illness of a partner, and the owner's desire to do something different.

There are many ways to find out which businesses are for sale. You may find advertisements in the local newspaper, or you may use a business broker. A **business broker** is a person who sells businesses for a living. People in your industry may know of businesses for sale. You may also find businesses for sale through other sources, including landlords and leasing agents, lawyers and bankers, management consultants, the Small Business Administration, Chamber of Commerce offices, and bankruptcy announcements.

## Advantages of Buying an Existing Business

There are many advantages of buying an existing business.

1. **The existing business already has customers, suppliers, and procedures.** The business may also have built up goodwill or customer loyalty. Of course, the new owner may want to change some of the policies and procedures established by the former owner. But fine-tuning systems that are already in place is likely to be much easier than creating systems from scratch.

2. **The seller of a business may train a new owner.** Also, experienced employees may be available to help the new owner learn about the company.

3. **There are prior records of revenues, expenses, and profits.** Having these records means that financial planning will be easier and more reliable than it would be for a completely new business.

4. **Financial arrangements can be easier.** The seller of the business may accept an initial partial payment and allow the rest to be paid off in monthly installments. This type of arrangement can reduce or eliminate the need for bank financing. If bank financing is needed, getting it may be easier because banks are more likely to lend to an established business.

**TEAMWORK**

In small groups, brainstorm a list of reasons business owners may decide to sell their businesses. Put a check mark next to the reasons that would affect the buyer's chance for success.

## Disadvantages of Buying an Existing Business

Buying an existing business sounds like an easy way to become an entrepreneur. However, buying a business can be risky.

1. **Many businesses are for sale because they are not making a profit.** Owners frequently try to sell businesses that are not financially viable.

2. **Serious problems may be inherited.** A business can have a poor reputation with customers, trouble with suppliers, or a poor location.

©iofoto, 2009/Used under license from Shutterstock.com

When it comes to customers, what are the advantages and disadvantages of buying an existing business?

**COMMUNICATE**

Use the Internet to research businesses for sale in your area. Make a list of five to seven questions you have about the sale of the business. Compose an e-mail to the seller asking for answers to your questions.

3. **Capital is required.** Many entrepreneurs just do not have the money to purchase a business. Starting a small business of their own may be their only option.

## Steps in Purchasing a Business

Buying a business is a complicated process that requires much thought. If you are considering buying a business, you will want to follow these steps.

1. **Write specific objectives about the kind of business you want to buy, and identify businesses for sale that meet your objectives.** Writing down your business objectives will help you find the right business for what you want to do.

2. **Meet with business sellers or brokers to investigate specific opportunities.** Ask about the history of the business, the reason it is for sale, its financial performance, and the price the owner is asking for the business.

3. **Visit during business hours to observe the company in action.** Inspect the facility closely to make sure that it meets your needs. Observe the number of customers who visit the business and how many make purchases. Look at the layout of the business.

4. **Ask the owner to provide you with a complete financial accounting of operations for at least the past three years.** Analyzing these reports will help you see how much profit you can make and how much you will probably be paying out in expenses.

5. **Ask for important information in written form.** Get a list of all assets to be transferred to the new owner, a statement about any past or pending legal action against the business, a copy of the business lease or mortgage, and a list of all the suppliers. Have an accountant and a lawyer help you review all of the material. Be suspicious if the owner refuses to provide all of the information you request.

6. **Determine how you would finance the business.** Contact lending institutions, and ask the seller if he or she would be willing to finance part or all of the purchase.

7. **Get expert help to determine a price to offer for the business.** An accountant or a **valuator**, an expert on determining the value of a business, can help. Present the offer in writing to the seller. If an agreement is reached, have a lawyer draw up a sales contract.

## CheckPOINT

What should you consider before purchasing an existing business?

_____

_____

# Enter a Family Business

The United States economy is dominated by family businesses. According to some estimates, as many as 90 percent of all businesses, including the vast majority of small- and medium-sized companies, are owned by families. Even many large companies, such as Chick-fil-A, continue to be owned and operated largely by people who are related to the company founder.

## Advantages of a Family Business

Entrepreneurs who work for their family businesses enjoy the pride and sense of mission that comes with being part of a family enterprise. They also enjoy the fact that their businesses remain in the family for at least one more generation. Some enjoy working with relatives. They also like knowing that their efforts are benefiting others whom they care about.

## Disadvantages of a Family Business

Family businesses have several drawbacks. Senior management positions are often held by family members, regardless of their ability. This situation sometimes means that poor business decisions are made. It also makes it difficult to retain good employees who are not members of the family. Family politics often enter into business decision making. Plus, the distinction between business life and private life is blurred in family-owned businesses. As a result, business problems end up affecting family life as well.

©Lisa F. Young, 2009/Used under license from Shutterstock.com

If you are not a family member, why might it be difficult to work in a family-owned business?

    Entrepreneurs who do join their family business must be prepared to make compromises. Unlike individuals who start or buy their own companies, people who work for their families lack the freedom to make all decisions themselves. They may also be unable to set policies and procedures as they would like.

## CheckPOINT

What are some of the advantages and disadvantages of entering a family business?

_____

_____

## Think Critically

1. When you purchase an existing business, why is it important to know the owner's reason for selling?

_____

_____

_____

2. What steps would you take when purchasing an existing business?

_____

_____

_____

3. What kind of information should you request before purchasing a business?

_____

_____

_____

4. Your family owns a successful business that distributes clothing from around the world to local retailers. Both your parents work full time in the business. They have offered you a position in the company after you graduate from college. Will you accept their offer? Why or why not?

_____

_____

_____

## Make Academic Connections

5. **Problem Solving** You purchased a company that makes and sells fine chocolates. You have a staff of 20 employees. As the new owner, you have noticed a lot of wasted product. You believe that some of the processes in use should be more efficient. Plan a meeting you will have with your employees to discuss this issue. Outline the agenda and describe your plan.

6. **Communication** Interview someone who owns a family business. Find out how long the business has been in operation and how many family members are employed in the business. Ask the owner what the advantages and disadvantages are of owning a family business. Compare this list to the advantages and disadvantages discussed in the text. Write a report on your findings.

**JUMP START**

After looking at existing businesses, Abbie and Kaito considered starting a new business. If they opened a new business, not only would they have to find a place to locate the bakery, but they would also have to buy everything needed to get started and build up a customer base. Another option they considered was buying a franchise for Mrs. Fields' Cookies. A franchise would offer help in finding a location and ordering supplies. But they wondered if they would be able to use some of their own recipes if they operated a franchise. What are some other questions to consider when starting a business or owning a franchise?

©Mike Neale, 2009/Used under license from Shutterstock.com

## Franchise Ownership

Purchasing a franchise is another route by which you can become an entrepreneur. Jiffy Lube stations are franchises. So are many McDonald's restaurants. Private entrepreneurs who operate them as their own businesses own these retail outlets.

A **franchise** is a legal agreement that gives an individual the right to market a company's products or services in a particular area. A *franchisee* is the person who purchases a franchise agreement. A *franchisor* is the person or company that offers a franchise for purchase.

More than 909,000 franchises are operating in the United States, and the number is growing. Franchising opportunities are available in virtually every field from motels to pet stores to video outlets. *The Franchise Opportunities Handbook*, a publication of the U.S. Department of Commerce, lists more than

1,400 franchise opportunities by category. It also provides information about costs and capital requirements. Sources for finding out about franchise opportunities include the following.

1. *Buying a Franchise: A Consumer Guide*, published by the Federal Trade Commission

2. Books on franchising available at your public library

3. *The Wall Street Journal*

4. Magazines such as *Forbes*, *Barron's*, *Entrepreneur*, and *Inc.*

## Operating Costs of a Franchise

If you decide to purchase a franchise, you will have to pay an initial franchise fee, startup costs, royalty fees, and advertising fees. You may also be asked to pay for nationwide advertising of the franchise.

The initial **franchise fee** is the fee the franchise owner pays in return for the right to run the franchise. The fee can run anywhere from a few thousand to a few hundred thousand dollars. It is usually nonrefundable. *Startup costs* are the costs associated with beginning a business. They include the costs of renting a facility, equipping the outlet, and purchasing inventory. A **royalty fee** is a weekly or monthly payment made by the owner of the franchise to the seller of the franchise. Royalty payments are usually a percentage of your franchise's income. *Advertising fees* are paid to support television, magazine, or other advertising of the franchise as a whole.

Jim Saurbrey purchased a Mr. Rooter franchise, a company that provides plumbing services. In return for the right to use the Mr. Rooter name and logo, Jim paid a franchise fee of $17,500. In addition to this fee, Jim spent $30,000 renting office space, leasing vehicles, and purchasing equipment.

During its first year of operation, Jim's franchise earned $36,000 in profits. He returned 4 percent of those earnings, or $1,440, to Mr. Rooter in royalty fees. During Jim's second year in business, his company earned $51,000. That year he paid $2,040 in royalty fees.

## Business Math Connection

Franchise operators often charge franchisees a percentage of sales as a royalty fee. If your sales totaled $5,600 in a month and the royalty is 10 percent a month, how much royalty fee would you pay?

**SOLUTION**
To calculate the royalty fee, multiply the sales by the royalty rate.

Sales × Royalty rate = Royalty fee

$5,600 × 0.10 = $560

The royalty fee would be $560.

## Advantages of Owning a Franchise

There are four main advantages to owning a franchise.

1. **An entrepreneur is provided with an established product or service.** This allows entrepreneurs to compete with giant companies.

2. **Franchisors offer management, technical, and other assistance.** This assistance can be onsite training or classes, aid with starting the new business and handling daily operations, and tips on crisis management. Some franchisors even offer help on everything from site selection and building design to equipment purchases and recipes. Most franchisors also maintain toll-free telephone numbers that franchisees can call for advice.

©Yuri Arcurs, 2009/Used under license from Shutterstock.com

What kind of assistance might franchisors offer?

## Cross-Cultural Relationships

### INTERNATIONAL FRANCHISES

Many entrepreneurs are finding franchising opportunities overseas. The key to success is finding the right fit. A country's customs and traditions must be taken into account. In the past, the lifestyles of foreigners were not always compatible with many U.S. business practices. But now, changing lifestyles have created unfulfilled needs that U.S. businesses can meet. For example, Home Instead Senior Care, which offers home care for senior citizens, has over 140 franchise locations in Japan. This is largely due to changing traditions that once dictated that aging parents be cared for by the women in the family. Now, many Japanese women have jobs outside the home, so families are looking for professional caregivers. Curves, a women-only fitness center, is also benefiting from Japan's changing lifestyles with over 740 franchise locations there.

### Think Critically

Why are international franchises becoming a popular way of doing business? What should an entrepreneur consider before expanding abroad?

3. **Equipment and supplies can be less expensive.** Because franchises are parts of large chains, they are able to purchase in huge quantities. Some of the savings they enjoy as bulk purchasers are passed on to the franchisee.

4. **A guarantee of consistency attracts customers.** Because a franchise contract mandates a certain level of quality, consumers know that they can walk into a franchise anywhere in the country and receive the same product or service. The cheeseburger sold at a Wendy's in Long Beach, California, will be very similar to the cheeseburger sold in Towson, Maryland. The quality of a room at a Ramada Inn in New Jersey will be much like the quality of a room at a Ramada Inn in Oregon.

## Disadvantages of Owning a Franchise

Although franchising sounds like a great idea, there are four main disadvantages you need to consider.

1. **Franchises can be expensive and cut down on profits.** The initial capital needed to purchase a franchise business often is high. Also, some of the profits you own as a franchise owner are returned to the franchisor as royalty fees.

2. **Owners of franchises have less freedom to make decisions than other entrepreneurs.** Many of the business decisions that entrepreneurs generally make themselves have already been made for franchisees. Franchisees must offer only certain products or services, and they must charge prices set by the franchisor. Many entrepreneurs object to this type of control because it inhibits the freedom they sought as independent business owners.

3. **Franchisees are dependent on the performance of other franchises in the chain.** A franchisee can benefit from the successes of other franchisees. But if other franchisees run sloppy operations, customer opinions of the chain will decline. As a result, customers may stop going to a franchise, even if a particular store maintains high standards.

4. **The franchisor can terminate the franchise agreement.** If the franchisee fails to pay royalty payments or to meet other conditions, the investment in the franchise can be lost. Similarly, when the franchise expires, the franchisor can choose not to renew the agreement.

©Frontpage, 2009/Used under license from Shutterstock.com

How can franchises be affected by other franchises in the chain?

## LOW-COST FRANCHISES

| Franchise | Description | Franchise Fee | Startup Costs | Royalty Fee |
|-----------|-------------|---------------|---------------|-------------|
| Instant Tax Service | Retail tax preparation | $39,000 | $39,000–$89,000 | 20% |
| Jani-King | Commercial cleaning service | $8,600–$16,300 | $11,300–$34,100 | 10% |
| Quiznos Subs | Submarine sandwiches, soups, and salads | $25,000 | $24,100–$341,800 | 7% |
| Kumon Math and Reading Centers | Supplemental education | $1,000 | $30,960–$129,400 | $30+/student/ month |
| Coffee News | Weekly newspaper distributed at restaurants | $6,000 | $9,400 | $20–$75/week |

## Evaluate a Franchise

There are many things to consider when purchasing a franchise. These are questions you should ask to evaluate a particular franchise.

1. What is the projected demand for the franchised product or service in the area in which I want to locate? Will I be guaranteed an exclusive territory for the duration of the franchise term, or can the franchisor sell additional franchises in the territory?

2. What are the costs and royalty fees associated with the franchise?

3. How profitable have other franchises in the area been? What do other franchisees think of the franchisor?

4. How long has the franchisor been in business? How profitable is the franchisor?

5. What services does the franchisor provide? Will the franchisor help me with marketing, merchandising, and site selection?

6. Are the benefits provided by the franchisor worth the loss of independence and the cost of purchasing the franchise?

7. What happens if I want to cancel the franchise agreement?

Some franchisors make false or misleading claims about their franchises. To make sure that you are not being cheated or misinformed, carefully study the documents the franchisor gives you. Be suspicious of any company that will not back up its claims with written financial statements. Also beware of high-pressure sales tactics. A franchisor that tries to get you to sign a franchise agreement right away is probably not offering you a good business opportunity. It is also a good idea to talk to other franchisees to learn about their experiences with the franchise. Do not commit to a franchise until you are completely sure of your decision. Never allow yourself to be pressured into making the decision too quickly.

Franchise agreements are complicated legal documents. Because they can be difficult to understand, you should never sign one without consulting an attorney. Let your attorney know what promises were made to you orally. Then ask your attorney to confirm that the same promises appear in the contract.

## Start Your Own Business

For one reason or another, running an existing business, joining a family business, or operating a franchise may not be possible for you, or it might not be right for you. This means that to be an entrepreneur, you will have to establish a business of your own. You need to consider the many advantages and disadvantages of starting your own business.

©SKdiz, 2009/Used under license from Shutterstock.com

What kind of decisions do entrepreneurs have to make when starting their own business?

### Advantages of Starting Your Own Business

Entrepreneurs who start their own business get to make decisions about everything from where to locate the business to how many employees to hire to what prices to charge. They are completely independent and decide their own destinies. Many entrepreneurs find enormous satisfaction in starting their own business. Many are attracted to the challenge of creating something entirely new. They also get a great feeling of triumph when their business turns a profit.

David Srivastava started his mail-order business, In a Jam, from his home. David started by selling dried fruit through the mail. After a year and a half of disappointing sales, David began offering preserves and jams, products he felt had greater sales potential. He also put more effort into packaging, and he designed the labels for the jars himself. His instincts proved correct: eight years after starting out alone in his basement, David now has accounts with several large retail stores, and his company has 14 full-time employees.

## Disadvantages of Starting Your Own Business

There are also many risks to consider when you start your own business. You must estimate demand for your product or service. There is no certainty that customers will purchase what you offer. Entrepreneurs who join family businesses, buy an existing business, or buy franchises do not have this uncertainty because it is already known that customers will buy the product or service.

Entrepreneurs who start their own business also must make decisions that other types of entrepreneurs need not make. What product or service to offer, the location, what employees to hire, and many other decisions must be made. The results of what may seem to be good decisions may not always be positive.

Lucy Chang realized how difficult it is to start a new business from scratch when she opened a kitchen accessories store. Lucy had considered purchasing a store franchise but had ruled it out because of the high franchise fee. Lucy's problems began when she discovered that her customers thought her location was inconvenient. As a result, fewer customers shopped in the store than Lucy had projected. Contacting suppliers was more difficult than Lucy anticipated, and many of them proved to be unreliable. The high-priced items Lucy purchased in the hope of increasing profits did not sell well.

©Raphael Daniaud, 2009/Used under license from Shutterstock.com

What risks does a new business owner face when making product decisions?

## CheckPOINT

Why do many entrepreneurs prefer to start new businesses rather than purchase existing businesses or franchises?

_____

_____

# Think Critically

1. What extra expenses could you expect to pay when operating a franchise as compared to operating a non-franchised company? Could you save money in expenses by operating a franchise? If so, how?

_____

_____

2. What are the advantages and disadvantages of owning a franchise? Do you think the advantages outweigh the disadvantages? Why or why not?

_____

_____

_____

_____

3. Do you think starting a business from scratch would be more challenging than buying an existing business or franchise? Why or why not?

_____

_____

4. In your opinion, what would be the greatest advantage of starting a new business? What would be its greatest disadvantage?

_____

_____

# Make Academic Connections

5. **Research** Identify a franchise that interests you. Research the franchise, and then evaluate the opportunity using the seven questions in this section. Write a short report on your findings. At the end of your report, explain whether you think this franchise is a good opportunity.

6. **Math** John and Molly Gonzales want to save enough money so that in five years they can purchase a cleaning service franchise. How much will they need to save each year if the franchise fee is $19,500 and startup costs are $15,200? (Do not consider interest earned on savings when calculating your answer.) If the company earns $24,700 in profits the first year, and the royalty fee is 6 percent, how much will the Gonzales' first royalty payment be?

7. **Communication** You are the owner of a coffee-shop franchise. The franchise agreement specifies that the franchisee must submit all advertising plans for approval. Write a memo to the franchisor outlining your plan to market the franchise's new bagels.

**JUMP START**

After careful consideration, Abbie and Kaito decided to start their own business. Now they had to decide what form of business ownership would work best for them. Abbie and Kaito could form a legal partnership and draw up a partnership agreement. But they also wanted to consider the advantages and disadvantages of incorporating their business because they liked the idea of limiting their liability. Someone suggested they look into incorporating as an S corporation. What advice would you give them?

## GOALS

**Compare a sole proprietorship and a partnership**

**Describe a corporation**

## KEY TERMS

**sole proprietorship,** p. 75

**partnership,** p. 75

**corporation,** p. 75

**share of stock,** p. 78

**board of directors,** p. 78

**dividends,** p. 78

**liability,** p. 79

## Forms of Business Ownership

Once you decide to start your own business, you must decide what type of ownership the business will have. There are three main types of ownership arrangements. A business that is owned exclusively by one person is a **sole proprietorship**. A business owned by two or more people is a **partnership**. A business with the legal rights of a person that is independent of its owners is a **corporation**. In addition, there are alternative forms of corporations.

## Sole Proprietorship

Sole proprietorships enable one person to be in control of all business aspects. Sole proprietorships may be very small businesses with just a few employees, or they may be large businesses with hundreds of employees.

**Advantages**  The government exercises very little control over sole proprietorships, so such businesses can be established and run very simply. Accurate tax records and certain employment laws must be met, but these are usually the only forms of government regulation on a sole proprietorship. For this reason, the sole proprietorship is by far the most common form of ownership in the United States.

**Disadvantages**  It can be difficult to raise money for a sole proprietorship. You are the only person contributing money to the business. Also, owners of sole proprietorships face a risk that owners of partnerships or corporations do not. If a sole proprietorship fails and debts remain, the entrepreneur's private assets may be taken to pay what is owed.

## Partnership

Many entrepreneurs prefer to go into business with one or more partners so that they have someone with whom to share decision-making and management responsibilities.

**Advantages**  Running a business as a partnership means that you will not have to come up with all of the capital alone. It also means that any losses the business incurs will be shared by all of the partners. Partners often offer different areas of expertise, which can strengthen the business. Like sole proprietorships, partnerships face very little government regulation.

**Disadvantages**  Some entrepreneurs do not like partnerships because they do not want to share responsibilities and profits with other people. They fear being held legally liable for the errors of their partners. Partnerships can also lead to disagreements and can end bitterly.

**Partnership Agreement**  When two or more entrepreneurs go into business together, they usually sign a *partnership agreement*, which sets down in writing the rights and responsibilities of each owner. It identifies the following.

1. Name of the business or partnership and names of the partners
2. Type and value of the investment each partner contributes
3. Managerial rights and responsibilities of each partner
4. Accounting methods to be used
5. Division of profits and losses among the partners
6. Salaries to be withdrawn by the partners
7. Duration of the partnership
8. Conditions under which the partnership can be dissolved
9. Distribution of assets upon dissolution of the partnership
10. Procedure for dealing with the death of a partner

**NETBookmark**

A partnership arises whenever two or more people co-own a business and share in the profits and losses of the business. Access www.cengage.com/school/business/21biz and click on the link for Chapter 3. Follow the link and read the article on partnerships. Then name and describe three common types of partnerships.

**www.cengage.com/school/business/21biz**

## GENERAL PARTNERSHIP AGREEMENT FORMING
## "SUNNY SIDE UP"

By agreement made this 21st day of September, 20--, we, Ana Ortiz, Keesha Gentry, and Thomas Chase, the undersigned, all of Palm Harbor, Florida, hereby join in general partnership to conduct a food service business and mutually agree to the following terms:

**1.** That the partnership shall be called "Sunny Side Up" and have its principal place of business at 2013 Sand Drive, Palm Harbor, Florida, at which address books containing the full and accurate records of partnership transactions shall be kept and be accessible to any partner at any reasonable time.

**2.** That the partnership shall continue in operation for an indefinite time until terminated by the death of a partner or by 90 days' notice provided by one or more of the partners and indicating his, her, or their desire to withdraw. Upon such notice, an accounting shall be conducted and a division of the partnership assets made unless a partner wishes to acquire the whole business by paying a price determined by an arbitrator whose selection shall be agreed to by all three partners. Said price shall include goodwill, and the paying of same shall entitle the payor to continue the partnership business under the same name.

**3.** That each partner shall contribute to the partnership: $22,000 for initial working capital and the supplies and equipment.

**4.** That in return for the capital contribution in item 3, each partner shall receive an undivided one-third interest in the partnership and its properties.

**5.** That a fund of $75,000 be set up and retained from the profits of the partnership business as a reserve fund. It being agreed that this fund shall be constituted on not less than 15 percent of the monthly profits until said amount has been accumulated.

**6.** That the profits of the business shall be divided equally among the partners, that the losses shall be attributed according to the subsequent agreement, and that a determination of said profits and losses shall be made and profit shares paid to each partner on a monthly basis.

**7.** That the partnership account shall be kept in the First Florida Bank and that all withdrawals from same shall be by check bearing the signature of at least one of the partners.

**8.** That each partner shall devote his or her full efforts to the partnership business and shall not engage in another business without the other partners' permission.

**9.** That no partner shall cause to issue any commercial paper or shall enter into any agreements representing the partnership outside the normal conduct of the food service business without notice to the remaining partners and the consent of at least one other partner and further that all managerial and personnel decisions not covered by another section of this agreement shall be made with the assent of at least two of the partners.

IN AGREEMENT HERETO, WE ARE

Ana Ortiz             Keesha Gentry             Thomas Chase

*Ana Ortiz*           *Keesha Gentry*           Thomas Chase

# Corporation

Unlike a sole proprietorship or a partnership, a corporation is treated independently of its owners. Since a corporation has the legal rights of a person, the corporation, not the owners, pays taxes, enters into contracts, and may be held liable for negligence.

## Corporation Basics

Ownership of a corporation is in the form of shares of stock. A **share of stock** is a unit of ownership in a corporation. People who own stock in the corporation are called *shareholders* or *stockholders*.

Every corporation has a **board of directors**, a group of people who meet several times a year to make important decisions affecting the company. The board of directors is responsible for electing the corporation's senior officers, determining their salaries, and setting the corporation's rules for conducting business. The board of directors also decides how much the corporation should pay in dividends. **Dividends** are distributions of profits to shareholders by corporations. The company's officers, not the board of directors, are responsible for the day-to-day management of the corporation.

What are the duties of the board of directors?

## Tech Literacy

### SOCIAL NETWORKING AND BUSINESS

E-mail has become a necessity for most business owners today to communicate with employees, shareholders, suppliers, and customers. Now social networking is entering the business scene. Business owners are beginning to find new and creative ways to use these sites for business promotion.

1. *Twitter* allows users to send very short messages called tweets that are no more than 140 characters long. Business owners find it a good way to keep their name in front of people who have a connection with or interest in their business. Some businesses also use it to announce special offers.

2. *LinkedIn* is a social networking site aimed specifically at business. It can be used to search for consultants and contractors. It has also become a major source for posting job openings.

3. *YouTube* is a great way to get information out to prospects and customers. You can make a short promotional video demonstrating your product or service or have current customers provide testimonials about it. A short e-mail can direct prospective customers to your YouTube video.

### THINK CRITICALLY

Why are social networking sites useful in business?

**Disadvantages** Setting up a corporation is more complicated than setting up a sole proprietorship or a partnership. To *incorporate* a business means to set up a business as a corporation. To incorporate, you will need the assistance of a lawyer, who will help you file articles of incorporation with the state official responsible for *chartering*, or registering, corporations. Because of this, establishing a corporation can be costly. Articles of incorporation must be written which fully detail the purpose of the business. If the articles are not well written, the corporations' activities can be limited.

Corporations are subject to much more government regulation than are sole proprietorships or partnerships. Another drawback of incorporation is that income is taxed twice. A corporation pays taxes on its income, and shareholders pay taxes on the dividends they receive from the corporation. This means that the corporation's profits are taxed as corporate income and again as individual income. This is known as *double taxation*.

**Advantages** If the corporate form of ownership is complicated and costly, why do entrepreneurs set up corporations? Liability is the main reason. Liability is the amount owed to others. The shareholders' liability is limited to the amount they invested when they purchased company stock.

Incorporation allows businesses to raise money by selling more stock. Lenders are also more willing to lend money to corporations than to sole proprietorships or partnerships. Finally, because shareholders do not participate in the management of a corporation, the top shareholder of the company can change, through the buying and selling of stock, without disrupting the day-to-day operation of the business.

### TEAMWORK

As a class, make a chart of the three legal forms of business ownership. List the advantages and disadvantages of each.

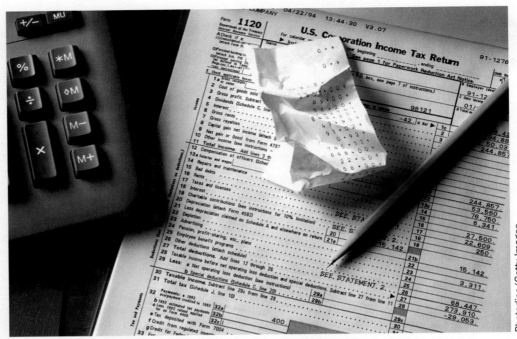

How are taxes handled for the various forms of corporations?

## S Corporation

Small corporations can elect to be treated as an S corporation. An *S corporation* is a corporation organized under Subchapter S of the Internal Revenue Code whose income is taxed as a partnership. Unlike regular corporations, an S corporation is not taxed as a business. Only, the individual shareholders are taxed on the profits (dividends) they earn. S corporations must follow the same formalities and record-keeping procedures as regular corporations. They are also managed by a board of directors and officers.

## Limited Liability Company

A *limited liability company (LLC)* is a legal form of business that goes further than an S corporation in providing the benefits of partnership taxation and limited personal liability for the owners of the business. The LLC is not subject to the rules for an S corporation, so it is simpler to operate. Owners of LLCs are known as members—not shareholders. Unlike shareholders, members can participate in the management of the business. The disadvantages of an LLC are that the type of businesses may be limited by state law, a single owner cannot establish an LLC, and many states limit the life of an LLC.

## CheckPOINT

What is the main benefit of setting up your business as a corporation?

_____

_____

# Think Critically

1. Which do you think is more risky: a sole proprietorship or a partnership? Explain your answer.

_____

_____

2. What would be the advantages and disadvantages of forming a partnership with a friend?

_____

_____

_____

3. Why do you think the government regulates corporations more closely than it does sole proprietorships or partnerships?

_____

_____

# Make Academic Connections

4. **Communication** With a partner, write a skit about two people who wish to form a partnership. Decide on a business to enter and the duties each person will perform in the business. In the skit, the partners should negotiate the terms of the partnership agreement.

5. **Math** Caren McHugh opened Best Foot Forward, a shoe store catering to women. To raise money, she organized as a corporation. She created 500 shares of stock, each worth $75. Caren holds 260 of the shares for herself. She sells the rest in even amounts to six investors. How many shares does each investor own? If Best Foot Forward fails and has $65,000 in debt, for how much would each investor be liable?

_____

_____

_____

_____

6. **Business Law** Create a chart comparing a sole proprietorship, a partnership, a corporation, an S corporation, and an LLC. Rate each legal form on the following: simple to start, decisions made by one person, low initial cost, limited liability, limited government regulation, ability to raise capital, and double taxation of profits.

## Chapter Summary

**3.1** **Run an Existing Business**

**A.** An existing business has an established customer base, relationships with suppliers, and records of profits made in the past. However, it may not be making a profit, or other problems may exist.

**B.** Joining a family business has advantages, such as pride in the business and enjoyment in working with relatives. But family politics can negatively affect the business and family life.

**3.2** **Own a Franchise or Start a Business**

**A.** Purchasing a franchise provides an established product or service for you to sell. But franchise ownership can be expensive, and it does not allow much room for independent decision making.

**B.** Creating an entirely new business offers complete independence and satisfaction. It can be risky because there is no guaranteed demand for your product or service.

**3.3** **Choose the Legal Form of Your Business**

**A.** A sole proprietorship is easy to establish and has only limited government regulation. However, it is difficult to raise money, and the owner faces risk of losing personal assets if the business fails. A partnership provides more capital, and financial losses are shared. Owners are legally liable for the other partners' errors.

**B.** A corporation is treated independently of its owners, has the legal rights of a person, offers limited liability to its owners, and can raise capital by selling more shares of stock.

## Vocabulary Builder

Choose the term that best fits the definition. Write the letter of the answer in the space provided. Some terms may not be used.

_____ 1. Weekly or monthly payment made by the owner of the franchise to the seller of the franchise

_____ 2. A business owned exclusively by one person

_____ 3. Group of people who meet several times a year to make important decisions affecting the company

_____ 4. A unit of ownership in a corporation

_____ 5. A person who sells businesses for a living

_____ 6. A business owned by two or more people

_____ 7. Distributions of profits to shareholders by corporations

_____ 8. A business with the legal rights of a person

_____ 9. A legal agreement that gives an individual the right to market a company's products or services in a particular area

_____ 10. The amount owed to others

**a.** board of directors

**b.** business broker

**c.** corporation

**d.** dividends

**e.** franchise

**f.** franchise fee

**g.** liability

**h.** partnership

**i.** royalty fee

**j.** share of stock

**k.** sole proprietorship

**l.** valuator

# Review Concepts

11. What are the advantages of buying an existing business? What are the disadvantages?

_____

_____

_____

_____

12. What are some of the compromises that must be made by an entrepreneur who joins the family business?

_____

_____

_____

13. Where can an entrepreneur obtain information about purchasing and operating a franchise?

_____

_____

_____

14. Why should an entrepreneur consult with an attorney prior to signing a franchise agreement?

_____

_____

_____

15. What kinds of decisions need to be made when starting a new business?

_____

_____

_____

16. What are the risks in starting your own business?

_____

_____

_____

17. Why do owners of sole proprietorships face more risks than owners of partnerships or corporations?

_____

_____

_____

**18.** What is the purpose of the partnership agreement?

_____

_____

**19.** What decisions does a corporation's board of directors make?

_____

_____

_____

**20.** What is the benefit of an S corporation? a limited liability company?

_____

_____

_____

## Apply What You Learned

**21.** You decide to start a business selling CDs over the Internet. What type of ownership will your business have (sole proprietorship, partnership, or corporation)? Why did you choose this form?

_____

_____

**22.** You are meeting with the owner of an ice cream shop you would like to purchase? What specific questions are you going to ask her? What documents do you want to see? How will you evaluate whether or not to purchase this business?

_____

_____

_____

**23.** Your family owns a successful restaurant. You are trying to persuade them to open another restaurant in a different part of town. What information will you present to persuade them to adopt your idea?

_____

_____

_____

**24.** The existing business you have purchased has trouble with suppliers. The previous owner did not pay them in a timely manner, and many of them refuse to ship goods to you on credit. What actions would you take to improve this situation?

_____

_____

_____

# Make Academic Connections

25. **Math**  You have purchased a car wash franchise. The franchise fee was $25,000. You must pay 6 percent of your earnings in royalty fees. In your first year, you paid $10,000 for equipment, $4,300 for operating costs, and $10,700 for part-time employees. Your first-year revenues were $120,000. Calculate the total expenditures for the first year. What was your profit? What will profits be in your second year if total revenues and costs remain the same? (Note: You do not need any new equipment.)

_____

_____

_____

26. **Research**  Use the newspaper, Internet, magazines and other materials to research business opportunities. Find a business for sale that interests you. Find out information about purchasing it. Include projected earnings and operating costs. If it is a franchise, include franchise fees and royalties. Do you think this would be a good investment? Why or why not?

27. **Communication**  You want to buy a clothing boutique. Write a letter to the owner of the store expressing your interest and requesting the necessary information you need to make a decision.

28. **Math**  Marta Vasquez is one of three partners in a car dealership. The division of profits and losses as specified in the partnership agreement is 60 percent for Marta, 25 percent for the second partner, and 15 percent for the third partner. The dealership has recently lost a lawsuit and must pay damages of $1,200,000. What is Marta's liability? What is the liability of each of the other two partners?

_____

_____

_____

29. **Business Law**  Use the Internet to learn how to form a corporation in your state. What are the requirements? What are the restrictions? How does the government regulate corporations? Write a one to two-page paper on your findings. Be prepared to share your report with the class.

# Ethical Dilemma

30. You have purchased a copy of the newest version of the Windows operating systems for the computers in your office. It was expensive for you to update your systems, but you felt it was important to keep your equipment up to date. Your friend, Jeff, who is a sole proprietor and is struggling to get his business going, really needs the new version of Windows, but he does not have the cash to pay for it. He asks you if you would mind sharing your software license with him. What would you do?

# Market Your Business

## Careers for Entrepreneurs

### LRMR

LeBron James is not content with just being a star on the basketball court. He also wants to become a leader in the global business world. He formed a sports marketing agency, LRMR Innovative Marketing and Branding, with three of his high school friends. In addition to turning James into a global icon, LRMR wants to "change the sports marketing prism through leveraging of sports, celebrity, and corporate infusion partnerships."

James wants to build a new financial model for the 21st-century athlete. He also formed King James, Inc., a holding company, to contract with endorsement partners and reduce tax liability.

Guiding principles that James has used in starting his business include

- Don't be afraid to ask for business advice
- Focus on unity rather than the individual
- Surround yourself with the best people
- Diversify income streams
- Remember that the brand is bigger than the man

### Think Critically

1. What do you think contributes to the success of LRMR?
2. Identify trends that you think could influence the success of LRMR.

# PROJECT | Marketing Your Business

## Project Objectives

- Analyze information about potential customers and competitors of your business
- Write the marketing plan for your business

©thumb, 2009/ Used under license from Shutterstock.com

## Getting Started

Read the Project Process below. Make a list of any materials you will need.

- Think about your business idea. If you were to start this business, who do you think your customers and competitors would be?
- As you develop a marketing plan, carefully analyze your marketing goals. Where do you see this business in one year? five years? ten years?

## Project Process

**4.1** Identify your target market and market segments. Use secondary data sources that could help you assess demand for your product or service. Develop a customer profile for your business.

**4.2** Conduct primary data research. Define the question—what it is that you want to learn from your research. Develop a survey and have at least 30 people in your target market fill it out. Analyze your results, and determine if your idea is feasible or if you need to make changes to it.

**4.3** Determine your competitors, both direct and indirect. Prepare a chart and analyze each competitor in terms of price, location, facility, strength, and weakness. Develop a customer loyalty plan.

**4.4 and 4.5** Write your marketing plan for the product, price, distribution, and promotion elements of the marketing mix.

## Chapter Review

**Project Wrap-up** Using a word processing program, key all the information that you have prepared in an attractive format. Add this to your business plan.

©Chin-Hong, Cheah, 2009/ Used under license from Shutterstock.com

**JUMP START**

Cheryl had always dreamed of having her own day spa business. She enrolled in the cosmetology program in high school, completed her training at the local technical college, and then got a job at a spa. After working for ten years, she told her friend Sergio about her idea of starting her own business. Sergio was very interested and told Cheryl that he and several of their coworkers would be interested in joining her. Cheryl realized that most of her clients would follow her to the new spa, but she didn't know if that would be enough to support the new business. She believed the spa would appeal to women and men between the ages of 23 and 50. They would be people who are concerned about their appearance, willing to pay extra for quality service, and have an average income of $35,000. She wanted to locate the spa in her community but was not certain there would be enough demand there. Why do you think it is important for Cheryl to know exactly who her customers are?

©Stephen Coburn, 2009/ Used under license from Shutterstock.com

## What Is Marketing?

As defined by the American Marketing Association, marketing is "an organizational function and a set of processes for creating, communicating, and delivering value to customers and for managing customer relationships in ways that benefit the organization and its stakeholders." To simplify this definition, **marketing** is all of the processes—planning, pricing, promoting, distributing, and selling—used to determine and satisfy the needs of customers and the company. This definition demonstrates the importance of the customer.

It is important to conduct market research to discover what products or services customers want to buy. Using data that is gathered through market research helps entrepreneurs develop a marketing concept for the business. The *marketing concept* uses the needs of customers as the primary focus during the planning, production, distribution, and promotion of a product or service. To use the marketing concept successfully, businesses must be able to

- Identify what will satisfy the customers' needs and wants
- Develop and market products or services that customers consider better than other choices
- Operate profitably

An important part of implementing the marketing concept is developing a marketing mix that helps meet customer needs and enables the business to earn a profit. The **marketing mix** is a blending of the product, price, distribution, and promotion used to reach a target market. For example, once you have determined what product or service meets customers' needs, you must determine the right price for it, make it available to the customers in the right places, and then let your target market know about it.

## CheckPOINT

How does the marketing mix for consumer products help meet consumer needs?

_____

_____

## Target Market

As an entrepreneur, you will need to estimate the demand for your products or services by identifying your primary customers. The **target market** includes the individuals or companies that are interested in a particular product or service and are willing and able to pay for it. Identifying your target market helps you reach the people to whom you most want to sell. Target customers are the customers you would most like to attract. A car dealer selling moderately priced minivans would target middle-class families with children. A car dealer that offers expensive sports cars might target single people with high incomes.

To identify the target market for your product or service, you will need to answer the following questions.

1. Who are my customers: individuals or companies?

2. If my customers are individuals, how old are they? How much money do they earn? Where do they live? How do they spend their time and money?

### TEAMWORK

Working with team members, look through magazines for an advertisement of a new product. Based on the type of publication and the material contained in the advertisement, answer the eight questions starting on this page about identifying a target market. Can you determine who the target market is for the product?

3. If my customers are companies, what industries are they in? Where are those industries located?

4. What needs or wants will my product or service satisfy?

5. How many potential customers live in the area in which I want to operate?

6. Where do these potential customers currently buy the products or services I want to sell them?

7. What price are they willing to pay for my products or services?

8. What can I do for my customers that other companies are not already doing for them?

## Understand the Competition

Knowing a lot about your competition will help you define your target market. Businesses enter into areas where there is competition all the time. However, they have to identify some special customer need or want that is not being met. Customers may be happy with the products or services being offered, but they may be unhappy with the prices being charged. Customers might be willing to pay more for better quality. In either case, a customer need is going unmet by a competitor, indicating a possible opportunity for an entrepreneur.

## Market Segments

To further define your target market, you need to identify market segments. *Market segments* are groups of customers who share common characteristics. Segmenting, or dividing your target market into several small groups, can help you develop a product or service that will meet customer needs. Market research can be used to identify market segments.

The process of market segmentation is important because most products and services only appeal to a small portion of the population. The leisure services market is a large market that includes many segments, such as outdoor adventurers, people who vacation frequently, and couples who eat at restaurants. Targeting the entire leisure market would not make sense. You would never be able to meet the needs of the entire market.

Creating a customer profile can be very useful in market segmentation. A *customer profile* is a description of the characteristics of the person or company that is likely to purchase a product or service. A customer profile can help you meet customer demand. Customers may be profiled based on many types of data, including demographics, psychographics, use-based data, and geographic data.

### SAMPLE CUSTOMER PROFILE FOR A SPORTING GOODS STORE

- Individual 23 to 52 years of age
- Participates in sports
- Wants good-quality sport equipment
- Looks for good prices
- Lives in city of Blanchester
- Average household income of $42,000 per year

©Nicholas Moore, 2009/ Used under license from Shutterstock.com

What kind of customer profile could you create from this group of people?

**Demographics** Data that describe a group of people in terms of their age, marital status, family size, ethnicity, gender, profession, education, and income are called *demographics*. An example of a market segment based on demographic data is women business owners between the ages of 25 and 40 who earn at least $50,000 per year.

**Psychographics** Data that describe a group of people in terms of their tastes, opinions, attitudes, personality traits, and lifestyle habits are called *psychographics*. An example of a market segment based on psychographic data is people who prefer to live in a downtown setting and whose musical preference is jazz.

**Use-Based Data** Data that help you determine how often potential customers use a particular service are called *use-based data*. If you were starting a travel agency, you would want to know how often potential customers travel.

**Geographic Data** Data that help you determine where your potential customers live and how far they will travel to do business are called *geographic data*. If you were thinking of opening a coffee shop, it would be important for you to know that people are not willing to drive more than one mile for coffee.

## CheckPOINT

How can creating a customer profile help entrepreneurs identify their target markets?

_____

_____

# Role of Market Research

For your business to succeed, you need to find out who your customers are, what they want or need, and how much they are willing to pay for your product or service. To collect this information, you will perform market research. **Market research** is a system for collecting, recording, and analyzing information about customers, competitors, goods, and services. You will draw on secondary data and primary data as you gather your information. Both types will help you identify ways to meet customer needs.

## Secondary Data

Entrepreneurs usually begin research of their target market by using secondary data. *Secondary data* is data found in already published sources. Information on population, family size, household income, economic trends, industry forecasts, and other information can be found in secondary data resources. Places to find secondary data include

1. Publications issued by government and community organizations, such as the U.S. Census, the Small Business Administration, and the Chamber of Commerce

2. Books about specific industries

3. Information on websites for government and businesses

4. Books about other entrepreneurs who set up similar businesses

5. Specialized magazines and journals devoted to particular fields

6. Newspaper articles and statistics

©David Gilder, 2009/ Used under license from Shutterstock.com

What websites might you visit to conduct market research for a new business?

## Primary Data

Most market researchers also collect primary data. *Primary data* is information collected for the very first time to fit a specific purpose. A researcher collects primary data to help identify and understand the target market. There are a few ways to collect primary data, such as through surveys, observation, and focus groups.

**Survey** The most common type of primary market research is a questionnaire or survey. A *survey* is a list of questions to ask your customers to find out demographic and psychographic information. A survey can be conducted by mail, over the phone, on the Internet, or in person.

### GLOBAL MARKETING

When planning to market products in other countries, it is important to be familiar with the values and practices of people in other cultures. It is also important to be sure that information is not translated incorrectly. Coca-Cola in China was first read as "Ke-kou-ke-la," meaning "bite the wax tadpole." Coke then researched 40,000 characters to find a phonetic equivalent, "Ko-kou-ko-le," translating into "happiness in the mouth."

### Think Critically

How can you familiarize yourself with different cultures?

**Observation** Market research can also involve observation. If you are considering opening a juice bar in a shopping mall, you might want to see how many customers you could attract. You could go to the mall and count the number of people purchasing drinks at various food outlets. An entrepreneur interested in starting a motorcycle shop might count the number of motorcycles going through a busy intersection.

**Focus Groups** Another way in which you could find out about the market is by conducting *focus groups*, which are in-depth interviews with small numbers of people. Groups of target customers are interviewed to gain valuable ideas on products or services. You can ask the same kinds of questions in a focus group that you would in a survey or questionnaire. The benefit of focus groups is that they allow for more in-depth discussion about a topic than a questionnaire does. Focus groups usually are led by a moderator who asks questions about buying habits, likes and dislikes, and interest in particular products and services. The focus group session is recorded so that the comments can be reviewed carefully after the session ends.

**Disadvantages of Primary Data** While primary data can provide the most up-to-date and useful information, it can be time-consuming and more expensive to gather than secondary data. You will need to determine how much secondary and primary market research data you need to collect.

## CheckPOINT

What is the difference between primary and secondary market research data?

_____

_____

## Think Critically

1. Why is it so important to determine who your target market is?

_____

_____

_____

2. How are market segments useful to an entrepreneur?

_____

_____

_____

3. Why do entrepreneurs need to conduct market research?

_____

_____

_____

4. You are thinking about opening a driving range and golf lesson center in your town. What type of secondary data should you consult? What type of primary data should you collect?

_____

_____

_____

_____

## Make Academic Connections

5. **Math** Marcel wants to open a car wash after graduating from high school. For several days, he observed the cars being washed at a competitor and recorded the information below. What is the average number of cars he counted each day? If his car wash were open five days a week, based on this data, how many cars might he expect to wash per year?

| Day | 1 | 2 | 3 | 4 | 5 | 6 |
|-----|----|----|----|----|----|----|
| Cars | 50 | 45 | 48 | 26 | 47 | 55 |

_____

_____

6. **Communication** Interview a business owner. Ask the owner the eight questions listed in the chapter for identifying a business's target market. Write a report based on what you find out about the owner's target market.

**GOALS**

Identify the six steps involved in primary data market research

Explain the importance of setting short-, medium-, and long-term goals for your marketing strategy

Describe the information that should be included in a marketing plan

**KEY TERMS**

marketing strategy, p. 98

marketing plan, p. 99

### JUMP START

After checking with the local Chamber of Commerce, Cheryl found that there is a population of over 500,000 and a median household income of $71,000 in her community. She believed the customer base was adequate, so her next step was to find out if the population would be interested in day spa services. Her friend Sergio suggested that she take a survey to find out what potential customers thought about her idea. What questions should Cheryl include in her survey to determine people's interest in her day spa?

## Six Steps of Market Research

Performing market research is vital to creating an effective marketing plan. Primary data market research is time-consuming and expensive, but it can uncover valuable information that you may not find in secondary data research. Primary data research involves six steps.

### 1. Define the Question

In the first step in the market research process, you should define exactly what you need to know. Entrepreneurs have many concerns and questions about the businesses they are planning. By determining what they need to know, they are defining the question that will be the focus of their research.

### 2. Determine the Data Needed

Once you have defined the market research question, you are ready to determine what data you need to collect to provide the answer to your question.

Entrepreneurs need to be sure that the data they collect will be helpful. By identifying the data needed, the data collection process will be more efficient.

## 3. Collect the Data

Before you begin collecting data, you need to decide how you will gather the data. The method you use will depend on what type of information you want to gather. For example, you can find out people's opinions in a survey or focus group, but not by observation. You should perform some secondary market research first to familiarize yourself with your market. Demographic and psychographic data and information on economic trends and industry forecasts will help you determine what kind of primary data research to perform.

If you use observation, you need to determine where and when to get the best information. With a focus group, you should think about what kinds of individuals to include and what questions to ask. If you choose a survey, think carefully about how long it should be, what questions it should include, how it should be administered, and how many people you should survey.

Making a good survey questionnaire is very important. Questionnaires should be kept to a page in length when read over the phone or mailed to respondents. Only questions that serve a specific purpose should be asked. A sample survey for a new dog-walking business is shown on the next page. It asks questions about the lifestyles, opinions, and choices of dog owners.

## 4. Analyze the Data

Once you have collected all your data, you need to analyze and interpret the information. The analysis should be in an organized format that it is meaningful and easy to study.

## 5. Take Action

Once you have analyzed and interpreted your data, you will need to determine how to use the data to make a decision. This is when you will develop a plan of action based on the information you found in your market research.

## 6. Evaluate the Results

It is not enough just to develop a plan of action. Entrepreneurs must regularly evaluate the effectiveness of the actions they take as a result of the plan to determine if any changes are needed.

### CheckPOINT

Why should you define the question you want your market research to answer?

_____

_____

# MARKET RESEARCH SURVEY

*Thank you for participating in this market research survey. We appreciate your assistance in helping us identify the needs of pet owners in our community.*

## PLEASE CHECK THE BOX THAT BEST DESCRIBES YOUR SITUATION.

Age: UNDER 18 ❑   19–30 ❑   31–40 ❑   41–50 ❑   51–65 ❑   OVER 65 ❑

Gender: MALE ❑   FEMALE ❑

Annual Household Income:

LESS THAN $25,000 ❑   $25,000–$50,000 ❑   $50,001–$100,000 ❑   MORE THAN $100,000 ❑

Number of pets: 0 ❑   1 ❑   2 ❑   3 ❑   4 OR MORE ❑

Kinds of pets: DOG ❑   CAT ❑   FISH ❑   BIRD ❑   OTHER ❑ (PLEASE SPECIFY)

IF YOU OWN A DOG, PLEASE ANSWER ALL OF THE FOLLOWING QUESTIONS.

How often do you walk your dog?

EVERY DAY ❑   A FEW TIMES A WEEK ❑   ONLY ON THE WEEKENDS ❑   NEVER ❑

OTHER ❑ (PLEASE SPECIFY)

Would you be willing to pay someone you trusted to take your dog for walks?

YES ❑   POSSIBLY ❑   NO ❑

How much would you be willing to pay to have your dog(s) walked for 30 minutes?

$10 ❑   $15 ❑   $20 ❑   $25 ❑   I WOULD NOT PAY TO HAVE MY DOG WALKED ❑

Who takes care of your dog when you are out of town?

KENNEL ❑   FRIEND ❑   NEIGHBOR ❑   OTHER ❑ (PLEASE SPECIFY)

Would you be interested in having someone you trust take care of your pets while you are away?

YES ❑   POSSIBLY ❑   NO ❑

## COMMUNICATE

Call your local Chamber of Commerce and ask them for information that would help the owner of a new dog-walking business that is opening in your town or city. Do not forget information on demographics and psychographics. Also, ask for statistics on dog ownership in your area. Write a report on your findings and present it to your class.

# The Marketing Strategy

As a business owner, you will need to outline the goals you want to accomplish through your marketing efforts. A **marketing strategy** is a plan that identifies how these goals will be achieved. Your strategy should address

- Product introduction or innovation
- Pricing
- Distribution
- Promotion
- Projected profitability
- Sales or market share

It is important that your marketing strategy be consistent with the overall goals you have set for your business. Your marketing goals should be written following the SMART guidelines (see Chapter 1). These goals should reflect your short-term, medium-term, and long-term plans for your business. Do you want to offer additional products or services after one year? Perhaps in five years, you want to sell your product internationally. Establishing short-, medium-, and long-term marketing goals ensures that the marketing you do today fits in with the vision you have for your business tomorrow.

## Short-Term Goals

Short-term goals are what you want your business to achieve in the next year. They can be stated in terms of number of customers, level of sales, level of profits, or other measures of success. Identifying your short-term goals will help you determine how to target your marketing. If your goal is to build a customer base, you may decide to keep prices low and spend money on promotion. If your goal is to have a positive cash flow, you may decide to price your products or services higher.

## Medium-Term Goals

Medium-term goals describe what you want to achieve in the next two to five years. Although your marketing strategy will be determined largely by your short-term goals, you will need to make sure that the strategy you are planning will make it possible to achieve your medium-term goals.

## Long-Term Goals

Long-term goals show where your business will be 5, 10, or even 20 years from now. Thinking about what you want to do in the long term can help you decide how to market the business today.

## CheckPOINT

Why is goal setting important when developing a marketing strategy?

_____

_____

# The Marketing Plan

After you have conducted your research and developed your marketing strategy, you will be ready to write your final marketing plan. The purpose of the **marketing plan** is to define your market, identify your customers and competitors, outline a strategy for attracting and keeping customers, and identify and anticipate change. A written marketing plan will help you determine whether it is solid and all parts are consistent. Your written plan becomes a guiding document as you operate your business. You can always review it later to determine if you need to change the way you are marketing your business. The marketing plan becomes a part of your business plan. Having a marketing plan as part of your business plan is essential when you seek financing for your business. Investors will expect your marketing plan to answer the following questions.

Why is it important to map out a marketing plan?

- What product or service will I offer?

- Who are my prospective customers?

- Is there a constant demand for this product or service?

- How many competitors are providing the same product or service?

- Can I create a demand for the product or service I want to offer?

- Can I compete effectively in price, quality, and delivery of my product or service?

To answer these questions effectively, the marketing plan for your business must include information on the following topics.

1. Product or Service
2. Target Market
3. Competition
4. Marketing Budget

5. Business Location
6. Pricing Strategy
7. Promotional Strategy
8. Distribution Strategy

As part of your marketing plan, you should include performance standards that will help you measure your effectiveness. After your marketing plan is implemented, you should compare your actual results to your performance standards to see how well you are progressing.

## CheckPOINT

Why is it important to put your marketing plan in writing?

_____

_____

## Think Critically

1. What are the limitations of primary market research?

_____

_____

_____

_____

2. Describe the six steps of market research in your own words.

_____

_____

_____

_____

_____

3. What makes a good questionnaire?

_____

_____

_____

_____

4. What is the relationship between short-, medium-, and long-term goals?

_____

_____

_____

_____

_____

## Make Academic Connections

5. **Problem Solving** Suppose your family-owned business processes and sells orange juice to food distributors. In order to grow, the business needs to add to its product line. On one page, discuss how to apply the six market research steps to help determine an additional product your business could offer.

6. **Communication** Write four more questions that the owner of the dog-walking business could have included in her survey shown on page 97. Also write why you think it would have benefited the business owner to ask these questions of her target market.

7. **Management** Choose one of the following businesses: Mexican restaurant, organic food store, advertising agency, or home improvement company. List short-, medium-, and long-term goals for the business.

### JUMP START

Cheryl's survey results indicated that there is a great deal of customer interest in a day spa in her community. As she prepared to proceed with her plans for the spa, Sergio suggested that Cheryl check out the other spas in the area to see what services they offer. Realizing the importance of competition, Cheryl knew that she would have to offer something different or better than the competition to attract customers to her spa. Also, once she got customers, she would have to do something to keep them coming back. She needed a customer loyalty plan. What could Cheryl do to make sure customers visit her spa instead of competitors' spas? What are some things she could do at her spa to establish customer loyalty?

**GOALS**

Explain the importance of understanding your competition

Discuss how to prepare a competitive analysis

Describe strategies for maintaining customer loyalty

**KEY TERMS**

direct competition, p. 102

indirect competition, p. 102

## Impact of Competition

The U.S. economic system is based on private property, freedom of choice, profit, and competition. Because consumers are free to buy whatever they want from whomever they want, companies compete for their business. Most new businesses face *competitors*—companies offering similar or identical products and services to the same group of target customers. As the owner of a new business, you will have to persuade customers to buy from you and not your competition. You must always watch the competition and be sure that you are offering products that are of equal or better quality at the same or lower prices.

Competitors may be categorized as either direct or indirect competition. You will need to find ways to identify and differentiate yourself from both types of competition.

## Direct Competition

**Direct competition** comes from a business that makes most of its money selling the same or similar products or services as another business. The Internet, telephone directory, and your local Chamber of Commerce can help you find direct competitors in your geographic area. Observation methods also can help you learn more about your direct competitors. If you start a retail business, you can visit all retail outlets in your area. Direct competition can be found in international markets as well.

## Indirect Competition

**Indirect competition** comes from a business that makes only a small amount of money selling the same or similar products or services as another business. Many businesses can compete with you indirectly. For example, a large department store may stock some of the same products carried by a small specialty shop. However, because sales of the products may comprise only a small amount of the department store's revenue, it is an indirect competitor.

## Large Retailers

When a large retailer enters a community, it can be a source of direct and indirect competition for many other businesses. Large retailers like Wal-Mart bring lower prices and jobs to a community, but many small businesses find it hard to compete. Some of the smaller, locally owned retailers often are forced out of business. Some of the reasons that it is difficult for entrepreneurs to compete with large retailers include the following.

1. *Large retailers usually are able to keep larger quantities of products in stock.* They can purchase inventory in larger amounts because they have more revenue and larger storage areas. Bigger orders result in volume discounts, and the savings can be passed on to consumers in the form of lower prices.

2. *Large retail chains do not rely on a single product line.* If one product line does poorly, the store does not go out of business because it has other successful product lines. Small businesses have risks associated with having only one product line if it falls out of favor with consumers.

3. *Large companies usually have more resources to devote to advertising.* A larger company makes more revenue and can hire advertising professionals to create effective advertising to attract more customers.

## CheckPOINT

What is the difference between direct and indirect competition?

_____

_____

_____

## Tech Literacy

### DO YOU NEED A WEBSITE?

In today's global economy, a well-designed website is almost essential for a successful business. Depending on your target market and the product or service you offer, your website will include different information. Basic information that should be available on your website includes the following.

- Information about your business and the products and services you offer

- Graphics, images, and photos that show your product and demonstrate its use

- Pricing information, including shipping costs

- Information on how to order online

- Contact information so that customers can contact you if they have questions about your products or services

### THINK CRITICALLY

What other things do you think a company website should include?

# Competitive Analysis

Identifying and examining the characteristics of a competing firm is called a *competitive analysis*. Analyzing the strengths and weaknesses of your competition will help you determine what you can do to get customers to buy from your business. Follow these steps to begin your competitive analysis.

Why should a new business owner visit the competition?

1. *Make a list of your competitors.* Using the Internet and *The Yellow Pages* and driving through the area in which you plan to locate your business are good ways to identify your competition. You can also talk to potential customers to find out with whom they are currently doing business. Review trade magazines and newspapers to see who is advertising the product or service you plan to offer.

2. *Summarize the products and prices offered by your competitors.* Investigate the products or services your competition offers for sale. How are they different from yours? Examine the price ranges of your competitors and determine how they compare to what you plan to charge. Are your prices higher or lower?

3. *List each competitor's strengths and weaknesses.* What does the competitor do that no one else does, or what does it do better than everyone else? Where are your competitors located? Determine if their location is better, worse, or about the same as the planned location for your business. Compare

the competitors' facilities to the planned facility for your business. Are their facilities better, worse, or about the same as yours? What attracts customers to your competitors' facilities? How will you compete with these strengths? What are some of the weaknesses of your competition? How can you use these weaknesses to your advantage?

4. *Find out the strategies and objectives of your competitors.* A copy of your competitors' annual report would have this information.

5. *Determine the strength of the market.* Is there an increase in demand for the product or service you plan to offer? Will there be enough customers for everyone in the market? What are the industry forecasts?

Interjit Singh wants to start a premier car wash in an expensive suburb of Washington, D.C. He does a competitive analysis as shown below and researches his direct and indirect competition. He finds that Royal Hand Wash is able to charge twice the price of the other competitors even though the location is not the best. Royal Hand Wash guarantees non-scratch car washes and waxes done by people, not machines. Because Interjit's business will also offer car washes, waxes, and detailing done by hand, Royal Hand Wash is the direct competition. All other car wash businesses, including gas stations with automatic car wash machines, are his indirect competition. Royal Hand Wash's location and prices are its biggest weaknesses, so Interjit plans to choose a prime location for his car wash and charge lower prices.

| ANALYSIS OF COMPETITORS | | | | | | |
|---|---|---|---|---|---|---|
| Competitor | Price | Location | Facility | Strength | Weakness | Strategy |
| Standard Gas | $6.00 | Excellent | Good | Excellent location | Car wash not easily accessible | Target a different market |
| Lakeland Car Wash | $5.50 | Fair | Good | Low price | Location | Target a different market |
| Ray's Car Wash | $5.00 | Good | Fair | Low price | Facility | Target a different market |
| Royal Hand Wash | $11.50 | Fair | Excellent | Excellent facility | Location, high price | Offer lower prices, better service, more convenient location |

## CheckPOINT

What is the purpose of a competitive analysis?

_____

_____

# Maintain Customer Loyalty

Getting customers to buy products or services from you and not your competition is only one step in running a successful business. You must also make sure your customers remain loyal to you. Loyalty develops because of positive experiences with a company or its products or services. Customers may like the prices, the quality of the products, the courteous staff, the location, or the superior customer service. Businesses must look for ways to strengthen customer loyalty because loyal customers are less likely to consider buying from competitors.

## Listen and Respond to Feedback

To keep customers, you will need to continually ask them questions about your company and respond to their feedback. Companies that ignore customer concerns will not stay in business long. Different companies stay in touch with their customers' needs in different ways. A cosmetics manufacturer may call customers the day after they receive a makeover to ask if they are happy with the products they purchased. Other companies have a customer feedback box where customers can put complaints or positive comments about the business. You can also design a survey for your customers to complete.

## Other Strategies for Maintaining Loyalty

To maintain customer loyalty, businesses use many strategies. The main purpose of these strategies is to keep customers happy so they keep coming back to your business. Some of the most basic strategies include

- Superior service
- More convenient hours than other businesses
- Easy return policies
- Store-specific credit cards
- Personal notes or cards for birthdays or a thank-you for their business
- Frequent buyer programs

## NETBookmark

Founded in 1981, San Francisco-based Kimpton Hotels & Restaurants are located throughout the United States and Canada. Kimpton InTouch is the chain's guest loyalty program. Access www.cengage.com/school/business/21biz and click on the link for Chapter 4 to answer the following questions: How much does it cost to become a Kimpton InTouch member? What are two ways InTouch members can earn complimentary night rewards? What other rewards can members earn?

**www.cengage.com/school/business/21biz**

---

## CheckPOINT

What are some strategies for maintaining customer loyalty?

_____

_____

# Think Critically

1. Why should entrepreneurs identify both direct and indirect competitors?

2. Why is a competitive analysis important to an entrepreneur?

3. Why can customer feedback be considered a type of market research? Is this market research more or less valuable than research you conduct? Explain your answer.

4. Why is it difficult for entrepreneurs to compete with large retailers?

# Make Academic Connections

5. **Management** Devise a plan to maintain customer loyalty for a hair salon. Create an advertisement to let your customers know about this plan.

6. **Communication** Shontel Washington just opened an art gallery. He would like feedback from the people who visit the gallery. Write a short questionnaire that would help Shontel learn more about his customers' feelings toward his business.

7. **Technology** Using the car wash data shown in the table on page 104, enter the prices into a spreadsheet. Use the spreadsheet to create a bar graph that will help the owner analyze the data.

**JUMP START**

As Cheryl prepared to open her spa, she was overwhelmed with the choices she had to make. In addition to a wide array of spa services, there were many products to choose from, including skin care, aromatherapy, and nail products, among others. Sergio recommended that Cheryl consider what products and services other spas in the area were offering. She might want her product mix to be a little different from her competitors. After determining what she wants to offer, Cheryl would have to decide who to purchase from and how to price the services and products. What suggestions do you have for Cheryl's product mix?

**GOALS**

Describe and define the importance of product features, branding, and positioning

Explain how to price products or services using various methods

**KEY TERMS**

product mix, p. 108

market share, p. 109

©Diego Cervo, 2009/ Used under license from Shutterstock.com

## The Product

Once you have determined what kind of business you will run, you will need to make decisions about the products that you will sell. Over the past 50 years, consumers have become more educated, and competition has increased to include the global market. This has led to a change in the U.S. market, from being a product-driven market to one that is consumer-driven. The marketing concept is the belief that the wants and needs of customers are the most important consideration when developing any product or marketing effort. The marketing concept can give small businesses an advantage over larger businesses because small businesses can be more responsive and more flexible when trying to satisfy customer needs.

## TEAMWORK

Working with team members, make a list of products and services you would offer if you were opening an extreme sporting goods store. Make a list of the features of your products and services. Write a positioning statement that differentiates your business from your competitors.

## Identify Your Product Mix

The different products and services a business sells are its **product mix**. In a consumer-driven economy, entrepreneurs realize that sometimes they must include products in their mix as a convenience for customers even though they may not be profitable. This will give the appearance to customers that the store has everything they need. It has been found that, often, a small percentage of the product selection makes up the majority of the sales revenue.

## Select Product Features

In addition to identifying your product mix, you will have to select product *features*, which are product characteristics that will satisfy customer needs. Every product has features. Features include color, size, and quality. They also include hours, warranties, delivery, and installation. You will need to consider your target market when selecting product features.

## Consider Branding, Packaging, and Labeling

Making your product stand out from all the others in the market is a challenging task. *Branding* is the name, symbol, or design used to identify your product. The package is the box, container, or wrapper in which the product is placed. The label is where information about the product is given on the package. The brand, package, and label that you choose for your product will help differentiate it from others on the market. When you see the Nike name and "swoosh" symbol, for example, you know about the quality of the product you have selected.

## Position Your Products or Services

Different products and services within the same category serve different customer needs. For example, both Hyundai and Jaguar sell automobiles, but these two products are positioned very differently in the marketplace. *Positioning* is creating an image for a product in the customer's mind. Businesses position a product in a certain market to get a desired customer response. Product features, price, and quality may be used for positioning. Jaguar's pricey cars are positioned for the person wanting high quality and status. Hyundai positions its product to satisfy a need for an inexpensive family motor vehicle. Examining the competition's positioning strategy can help you determine the best positioning strategy for your target market.

## CheckPOINT

Why are product features, branding, and positioning important?

_____

_____

# Price

The price is the actual amount a customer pays for a product or service. Prices you charge must be low enough so that customers will buy from you and not from your competitors. To earn a profit, though, your prices need to be high enough so that revenues exceed expenses.

## Set Pricing Objectives

Before you can select a pricing strategy, you will need to establish objectives for your pricing program. What is the most important thing you want the price to do? Examples of price objectives include

- Maximize sales
- Increase profits
- Discourage competition
- Attract customers
- Establish an image

## Consider the Return on Investment

When setting pricing objectives, you may want to consider your return on investment. Investment refers to the costs of making and marketing a product. The *return on investment (ROI)* is the amount earned as a result of the investment, usually expressed as a percentage. Entrepreneurs must identify the percentage return they want from their investment. The target percentage in the beginning may be lower than it will be as the business grows. If you invest $5,000 in your smoothie stand and you want a 15 percent return, you need to price your product so that you will earn $750, since $5,000 × 0.15 = $750.

What factors must be considered when setting a price for a product?

## Determine the Market Share

Market share is a business's percentage of the total sales generated by all companies in the same market. For example, if people in a specific community normally spend $1,750,000 a year on gourmet food products and a gourmet food store's sales are $192,500, its market share will be 11 percent.

| Amount of sales | ÷ | Total market size | = | Market share |
|---|---|---|---|---|
| $192,500 | ÷ | $1,750,000 | = | 11% |

Your market share will depend on the level of competition in your market. You can increase market share by lowering prices. Advertising and promotion campaigns that attract more customers can help too. You also can network with potential customers. *Networking* involves establishing informal ties with people who can help your business grow. Attending trade association meetings and other gatherings can provide good networking opportunities.

## Price a Product

Once pricing objectives have been determined, the next step is to determine the possible prices for products. There will usually be more than one price that can be charged for a product. Pricing may be based on demand, cost, or the amount of competition.

**Demand-Based Pricing** Pricing that is determined by how much customers are willing to pay for a product or service is called *demand-based pricing*. Potential customers are surveyed to find out what they would be willing to pay. The highest price identified is the maximum price that can be charged.

**Cost-Based Pricing** Pricing that is determined by using the wholesale cost of an item as the basis for the price charged is called *cost-based pricing*. A *markup price* is the retail price determined by adding a percentage amount to the wholesale cost of an item.

Sometimes business owners purchase too much of a particular item and want to sell more of it quickly. To do so, they mark down the retail price of the product. A *markdown price* is a price determined by subtracting a percentage amount from the retail price of an item. You should be careful not to mark down an item below its cost. You do not want to lose money.

**Competition-Based Pricing** Pricing that is determined by considering what competitors charge for the same good or service is called *competition-based pricing*. Once you find out what your competition charges for an item, you must decide whether to charge the same price, slightly more, or slightly less.

## Business Math Connection

If Luisa Ramirez, a gourmet food store owner, buys artichoke hearts for $1.77 a can and wants to add 40 percent to the wholesale cost, what would the retail (markup) price be? If Luisa usually sells olive oil for $10.50 a bottle and wants to mark down the price 20 percent to try to sell more olive oil, what would the markdown price be?

**SOLUTION**
Use the following formulas to calculate retail price.

Wholesale cost × Percentage markup = Markup amount
$1.77 × 0.40 = $0.71

Wholesale cost + Markup amount = Retail price
$1.77 + $0.71 = $2.48

Use the following formulas to calculate markdown price.

Retail price × Percentage markdown = Markdown amount
$10.50 × 0.20 = $2.10

Retail price − Markdown amount = Markdown price
$10.50 − $2.10 = $8.40

## Price a Service

When setting the price for a service, it is important to consider not only the cost of any items used in providing the service but also the amount of time involved and anything that is included with the service.

**Time-Based Pricing** The price to charge for services can be determined by the amount of time it takes to complete the service. A plumber may charge $100 per hour. If the job takes 1½ hours to complete, the labor charge would be $100 × 1.5 = $150. A service provider must decide whether there will be a separate charge for materials or whether the materials will be included. A hair stylist charges a set amount to highlight someone's hair. The amount includes the hair stylist's time as well as all of the supplies used for the highlighting. Some service providers will negotiate the price. This is often done with legal services and construction projects.

©Lisa F. Young, 2009/ Used under license from Shutterstock.com

How is pricing a service different from pricing a product?

**Bundling** Services can be *bundled*, or combined under one price, rather than making the customer pay for each individual part of the service. Airlines use bundling when they charge a passenger for a ticket. The price includes not only the transportation, but also any food and beverages served in flight, the services of the employees who check in passengers, and baggage handling.

## Pricing Techniques

It is important to set the right price for your products and services. Pricing can make or break a business. Different techniques may be used to set prices at different stages of the business.

**Introductory Pricing** As a product is introduced into the market, sales will be low, marketing costs will be high, and little if any profit will be made. Two introductory pricing techniques are price skimming and penetration pricing. *Price skimming* is used when a product is new and unique. A high price is charged to recover the costs involved in developing the product. Then as more competitors enter the market with similar products, the price is dropped. *Penetration pricing* starts out with a low introductory price with the goal of building a strong customer base. The low price also discourages competition.

**Psychological Pricing** Pricing based on the belief that certain prices have an impact on how customers perceive a product is called *psychological pricing*. Techniques used in psychological pricing include the following.

- *Prestige pricing* is selling at a high price in order to create a feeling of superior quality and social status.

- *Odd/even pricing* suggests that buyers are more sensitive to certain ending numbers. Studies have shown that prices ending in odd numbers are perceived to be bargains while those ending in even numbers suggest higher quality. For example, a shirt that sells for $29.99 sounds like a bargain compared to one that sells for an even $30.00.

- *Price lining* involves offering different levels of prices for a specific category of product based on features and quality. A jeweler might offer three price lines of diamond necklaces and display them in different cases so that shoppers can go straight to the price level they can afford.

- *Promotional pricing* is offering lower prices for a limited time to increase sales. This type of pricing is temporary, and prices will return to normal when the promotion ends.

- *Multiple-unit pricing* involves pricing items in multiples, such as 10 for $10. This type of pricing suggests a bargain. People will buy more items than they would if they were priced individually.

**Discount Pricing** Pricing that offers customers a reduced price is *discount pricing*. It is used to encourage customers to buy. Markdowns are a type of discount pricing. Other discount pricing strategies include the following.

- *Cash discounts* are offered to customers to encourage early payment of invoices. When this is done, the terms of an invoice will include the amount of the discount, the number of days in the discount period, and when the invoice is due if the discount is not taken. For example, terms of "2/10, net 30" mean that a 2 percent discount may be taken if the invoice is paid within 10 days. If no discount is taken, the net or total amount of the invoice is due within 30 days of the date of the invoice.

- *Quantity discounts* are reductions in price based on the purchase of a large quantity. This is also called a volume discount. Sellers offer quantity discounts because they reduce their selling expenses.

- *Trade discounts* are reductions on the list price granted by a manufacturer or wholesaler to buyers in the same trade.

- *Seasonal discounts* are used for selling seasonal merchandise out of season. For example, barbecue grills are in high demand in the spring and summer months, but not in the fall and winter. Manufacturers offer discounts to customers who purchase grills out of season.

## CheckPOINT

What pricing objectives are most important to a new business?

_____

_____

# Think Critically

1. In the blue jeans market, which brands are positioned to satisfy customers' need for high quality and status? Which brands are positioned to satisfy a need for inexpensive clothing? Describe the consumers who are more likely to buy each of the brands you name.

_____

_____

_____

_____

2. What do you need to consider when pricing services?

_____

_____

_____

_____

3. Which method of pricing do you think is most effective? Why?

_____

_____

_____

_____

# Make Academic Connections

4. **Communication** Look through advertisements in newspapers and magazines and find examples of psychological pricing. Prepare a poster of the advertisements and label each pricing technique.

5. **Math** A shoe store owner pays a manufacturer $54 a pair for a popular brand of athletic shoes. The store offers the shoe to customers for $129 a pair. What is the markup percentage? The shoe store owner decides that the shoes are not selling quickly enough. The store has a sale offering a 30 percent markdown on the shoes. What is the sale price?

_____

_____

_____

6. **Problem Solving** Your sporting goods store sells fitness equipment. Included in your product mix is a treadmill that is not selling well, and you do not understand why. List some possible causes. Outline strategies for determining the reasons behind low sales.

### GOALS

Explain the difference in the channels of distribution and determine which is appropriate for different businesses

Evaluate different types of promotion tools

### KEY TERMS

channels of distribution, p. 114

advertising, p. 117

publicity, p. 120

 **JUMP START**

As Cheryl continued planning for the opening of her day spa, she turned her attention to the distribution and promotion elements of the marketing mix. She realized that as a service provider, she would sell her services directly to her customers. However, she would have to consider distribution methods for the supplies she would use and the products she would sell at her business to ensure she had everything when she needed it. As for promoting her business, Cheryl decided to place a newspaper ad and host an open house to celebrate her grand opening. She knew there were many other ways she could promote her business. What recommendations would you make to Cheryl about distribution and promotion?

Photodisc/Getty Images

## Distribution

Distribution is an important component of the marketing mix that involves the locations and methods used to make products available to customers. As you develop a distribution strategy for your business, you will determine how you will get your goods and services to your customers. You must be sure you have the right product in the right place at the right time.

**Channels of distribution** are the routes that products and services take from the time they are produced to the time they are consumed. Choosing the right channel of distribution for a product includes finding the most efficient way to ship it to desired locations. Using the right distribution channels saves time and lowers costs for both buyers and sellers.

## Direct and Indirect Channels

Channels are either direct or indirect. A *direct channel* moves the product directly from the manufacturer to the consumer. An *indirect channel* uses *intermediaries*—people or businesses that move products between the manufacturer and the consumer. Agents and wholesalers serve as intermediaries.

## Channel Options

**TEAMWORK**

In small groups, draw flow charts tracing all the channels of distribution possible for one of the following products: apples, calculators, magazines, milk, or motor oil.

Entrepreneurs should examine the different options for channels of distribution and choose the one that best meets the needs of their business and customers. The four basic options are illustrated and described below.

1. **Manufacturer to Consumer** The product can be sold by the manufacturer directly to the consumer through the Internet, direct mail, or television shopping channels. There are no intermediaries involved, and this option is the most cost-effective. However, sales opportunities are limited because it is more difficult for a manufacturer to reach the final consumer.

2. **Manufacturer to Retailer to Consumer** A sales force can sell manufactured goods to retail stores, and the retail stores can sell to the consumers. This option is more expensive than selling directly from the manufacturer to the consumer, but it offers more sales opportunities.

3. **Manufacturer to Wholesaler to Retailer to Consumer** To reach a large market, the manufacturer can sell large quantities to a wholesaler who will then store and sell smaller quantities to many retailers. Even though more intermediaries are involved in this method, prices can be lower because the manufacturer is producing mass quantities of the product, resulting in lower production costs.

4. **Manufacturer to Agent to Wholesaler to Retailer to Consumer** With this option, the manufacturer does not get involved in selling. Selling is handled by an agent. This option is often chosen by manufacturers involved in international marketing.

## Distribute Goods and Services

Retail, service, and manufacturing businesses will choose different channels of distribution based on the needs of their businesses. All types of businesses must carefully plan their distribution strategy to ensure customer satisfaction.

**Retail Businesses** A retail business has many ways of selling products. As the owner of a retail business, you can distribute products in various ways.

- Offer your product or service to consumers in a convenient location and during convenient hours.

- Use catalogs, fliers, and other advertisements to reach customers who live outside the area. Ship phone or fax orders directly to customers.

- Create a website. People with access to the Internet can visit your website to learn about your products and services and to make purchases.

**Service Businesses** Most entrepreneurs who own service businesses sell their services directly to customers. These businesses have a single, direct channel of distribution because the production and consumption of a service happens at the same time. For example, electricians, restaurant owners, and lawyers deal directly with the people who purchase their services. Some service businesses, such as film developers, use retail stores to distribute their services.

**Manufacturing Businesses** Manufacturers usually do not sell directly to customers. Instead, they make their products and then sell them to other businesses, such as retailers. The retail store then sells to the final consumer.

Some manufacturers distribute their products very broadly and use all possible channels of distribution. Other manufacturers distribute their products through selected outlets only. For example, high-priced cosmetics usually are sold in exclusive department stores. Inexpensive cosmetics are sold in discount stores and drugstores.

## Physical Distribution

All types of businesses must receive goods from suppliers. Whether or not they sell goods to customers, all businesses need paper, computers, raw materials, and more to be able to function. Retail businesses need to obtain goods to sell. Regardless of the type of business, distribution needs must be considered.

Physical distribution includes not only transportation but also storage, handling, and packaging of products within a channel of distribution. A product may move through several channel members by various forms of transportation to get it to the point where it will ultimately be sold to consumers. As the product is transported, it will be stored at points along the channel as paperwork is processed and it is moved to the next channel member. To protect the product, storage facilities along the channel must be adequate and safe.

**Transportation** Products can be moved by airplane, pipeline, railroad, ship, truck, or a combination of methods. You must determine which method is best and most cost-efficient for your products. Factors to consider in making a transportation decision include what you are shipping and where it is being shipped. If you are shipping a small product to someone in your city, you would probably choose a parcel delivery service. If you are shipping a large item to another country, you would probably send

©Michael Shake, 2009/ Used under license from Shutterstock.com

Why do business owners need to carefully select the mode of transportation used for delivery of products?

the item by ship or air and use a truck to get the product to and from the shipyard or airport. If the product is perishable, you may need to choose a carrier that provides refrigeration or that can move the product very quickly to its destination.

**Product Storage and Handling** Efficient storage allows channel members to balance supply and demand of products. However, this adds to the cost of the products and also adds the risk that products may be damaged or stolen while stored. Most products are stored in warehouses at various points through the channels of distribution.

**Packaging** Packaging is designed to protect the product from the time it is produced until it is consumed. If the product is not protected during the distribution phase, it could be damaged or destroyed, resulting in a loss of money to channel members. Packaging requirements will vary depending on the product, the way it is shipped, and where it is being shipped.

---

## CheckPOINT

Why are channels of distribution different for different types of businesses?

_____

_____

---

# Promotion

You will have to promote your business to make customers aware of the benefits of buying from you. Promotion takes many forms, including advertising, publicity, personal selling, and sales promotion. The strategy created by adopting a blend of some, if not all, of these techniques is called your *promotional mix*. Once you determine your promotional mix, you must obtain the approximate costs for all forms of advertising media that you plan to use and determine whether this budget is realistic for your business.

## Advertising

Service industries, manufacturers, and retailers all advertise. **Advertising** is a paid form of communication sent out by a business about a product or service.

Your advertising should clearly communicate the message and image you want to convey. If, for example, your marketing strategy is to have low prices, advertisements highlighting your prices might be appropriate. If your aim is to target customers who are willing to pay higher prices for excellent service, advertising that describes your well-trained staff would fit your image.

Once you choose a message, you will need to decide which advertising medium to use. To choose a medium, you will have to consider both cost and effectiveness in reaching your target audience.

**Online Advertising** As Internet use has increased, online advertising has become widely used by businesses to promote their products and services. This is a cost-effective way for businesses to get information to potential customers. It allows potential customers to use keyword searches and to browse through online catalogs by category to find available products and services.

Online advertising does have some disadvantages. Many marketers have abused the Internet and its ease of use with excessive *spamming*—sending mass mailings by e-mail to Internet users. Excessive use of pop-ups, flashy banners, and spam has caused people to use software to block promotions.

**Television Advertising** Promotions on television are the best way to reach a large number of people quickly. Television advertising comes in the form of commercials and paid advertisements. Commercials are usually less than a minute in length and are run during breaks in television programming. They are very short promotions about a product or business. Paid advertisements—also known as infomercials—can last a half hour or more and go into depth about the product being offered.

Television advertising expenses include the fee you have to pay the station, which is based on the amount of time your advertisement or commercial plays. You also must consider the costs of producing the commercial. If a one-minute commercial costs $25,000 to produce, you pay the television station $2,000 for each minute it airs, and you plan to have it aired 30 times, the cost per minute would be [$25,000 + ($2,000 × 30)] ÷ 30 = $2,833.33.

Television advertising can be very expensive. Producing even a low-budget commercial can cost thousands of dollars. You will need the help of video and production professionals when developing a television ad. You also will have to pay a network or cable station to broadcast the commercial.

Television reaches too broad an audience to be effective for most businesses. If, for example, only one percent of the audience is interested in a particular product, advertising on television is not likely to be cost-effective.

**Radio Advertising** Radio advertising can be effective for small businesses. It is less expensive than television promotion. You can also be more certain you are reaching your target market. Radio stations tend to attract a particular kind of listener. Pop rock stations target teenagers and people in their twenties. Classical or talk radio stations usually attract older listeners. Selecting a station whose listeners share the same demographics as your target market can increase the effectiveness of your advertising. You can contact stations and ask for a demographic profile of their listeners.

The costs of radio advertising are determined in the same way as the costs of television advertising. You must pay for air time and production costs.

A disadvantage of radio advertising is that radio is a purely audio message, and it cannot visually show your product. Radio listeners may tune out or even "surf the airwaves" during the commercial spots. You also may need professional help when developing a radio ad, which can be costly.

**Newspaper Advertising** Newspapers have been the single largest form of advertising in the United States. However, as more people are looking to the Internet for news and information, newspaper circulation has dropped in many cities. Small businesses may choose to promote their products and services in the newspaper because it is relatively inexpensive, it targets a limited geographic area, and it reaches large numbers of people.

As with other forms of advertising, there are some disadvantages of newspapers. Newspapers reach a large audience, but much of that audience may not be interested in your business. Another disadvantage of newspaper advertising is the fact that newspapers carry so many advertisements that readers may overlook yours.

**Telephone Directory Advertising** Telephone directories list the phone numbers of people and businesses in a certain area. Directory ads usually appear on a page close to the listing of the business placing the ad. Directory ads can be similar in appearance to newspaper ads. Customers look in telephone directories again and again, making them a good advertising medium.

A disadvantage of directory advertising is that people look in the directory only when they are already in search of a particular type of business. With directory advertising, it is not easy to persuade customers to try your business instead of a competitor's.

Why are newspaper ads a popular way to promote a business?

**Direct-Mail Advertising** Direct-mail advertising includes fliers, catalogs, letters, and other correspondence sent to target customers through the mail. Mailing lists for target markets are available for purchase. If your business sells hospital beds, you can purchase targeted mailing lists of people who would purchase your product. You can also get lists of people based on the geographic area. Companies that specialize in maintaining targeted mailing lists can provide almost any kind of list for any kind of business.

Direct-mail advertising can be effective if people read it, but many people throw out direct-mail advertising, calling it "junk mail." If you use this method of advertising, you will want to come up with an attention-grabbing design or other means of making people want to read it.

**Magazine Advertising** Magazines are an excellent way to aim products and services at specific markets. Fitness magazines are full of advertisements for athletic equipment. Magazines targeting teenage girls are full of advertisements for products that appeal to them, such as cosmetics and clothing.

Most magazines are nationally distributed. This can make them inappropriate for businesses that sell in a limited geographic area. Some cities have local magazines, which would be an effective way to target a certain area.

**Outdoor Advertising** Outdoor advertising includes billboards and signs. Such advertising can be effective in keeping the name of your business in a place where many people can see it. But because people view such advertising quickly as they drive by, it cannot include much information. Also, outdoor advertising may not project the image your business is trying to convey.

**Transit Advertising** Transit advertising consists of signs on public transportation. Transit advertising can provide more information than is typically seen on a billboard. Such advertising can be effective if the market you are trying to reach includes many people who use public transportation.

## Publicity

**Publicity** is a nonpaid form of communication that calls attention to your business through media coverage. Good publicity can be as helpful as advertising. Publicity is free, but staging an event or bringing in a celebrity to generate publicity usually is not. While there are things you can do to attract positive media attention, publicity is largely out of your control. Publicity can be negative if the media coverage is unfavorable. One form of publicity is a *press release*, which is a written statement to inform the media of an event or product. An example of a press release is shown here.

## Other Types of Promotion

Advertising and publicity are not the only ways to promote your business. You can offer sales promotions or use personal selling.

*Sales promotion* is the act of offering an incentive to customers in order to increase sales. Examples of sales promotion include contests, free samples, coupons, rebates, frequent purchaser programs, and special events.

Some companies offer rebates. A *rebate* is a refund offered to people who purchase a product. For example, customers who purchase a $12 bottle of olive oil may be entitled to a $2 rebate from the manufacturer.

*Personal selling* is direct communication between a prospective buyer and a sales representative. The sales representative attempts to persuade the prospective buyer to make a purchase. Being courteous, knowledgeable, and available to customers will reflect positively on your business.

*Telemarketing* is using the phone to market your product or service. It can be a cheap, effective way to let people know about your business or about special offers. Keep in mind that some consumers consider telemarketing to be annoying and would rather not be contacted at home.

---

**FOR IMMEDIATE RELEASE**

GALA OPENING OF LUISA'S GOURMET LUXURIES

Come celebrate the opening of Luisa's Gourmet Luxuries on Friday, September 20, at 8:00 p.m. Hors d'oeuvres, imported champagne, and French pastries will be served at the event. Music will be provided by Glendale's leading jazz ensemble, Jazz Expressions.

The opening of Luisa's Gourmet Luxuries marks the realization of a dream by owner Luisa Ramirez. "As a specialty cook," she says, "I could not always find the products I needed. And I was never happy with the selection of produce and baked goods in town." Luisa decided to open a store that would offer the kinds of products she could not find elsewhere in town.

Luisa's Gourmet Luxuries offers an astounding selection of products, including 14 different kinds of olive oil, 12 different kinds of rice, and pasta products from several different countries. "Everyone's tastes are different," says Luisa, "so I offer a large selection."

For more information, contact:

Luisa Ramirez, Proprietor
Luisa's Gourmet Luxuries
1610 Marbury Road, Glendale, CT
(275) 555-3983

---

## CheckPOINT

Describe the differences among advertising, publicity, and sales promotions.

_____

_____

# Think Critically

1. Why is advertising important for a new business?

_____

_____

_____

2. Describe some publicity activities or events that businesses in your area have held.

_____

_____

_____

3. How would you decide which of the ways to advertise is the best and most cost-effective choice for your business?

_____

_____

_____

4. You are going to open a retail store that will offer gifts and accessories. Your target market is 13- to 15-year-old girls. Describe the promotional mix you will use for your business.

_____

_____

_____

# Make Academic Connections

5. **Communication** Write a paragraph explaining all the possible channels of distribution for a T-shirt manufacturer.

6. **Geography** Think of a product that would have to be shipped from another country to the United States. Research the route that the product would follow while being shipped. Write a paragraph describing the places the product would pass through and describe the method(s) of transportation that would be used for shipping.

7. **Problem Solving** You are opening a new gardening service business in your community. You will help your customers plan their flower and vegetable gardens and shop for their plants. You will also provide planting services if your customers need them. Describe all of the promotional activities that you will plan for the business. Write a press release to inform the local media about the opening.

# CHAPTER 4 — ASSESSMENT

## Chapter Summary

### 4.1 The Value of Marketing
A. Marketing is used to determine and satisfy the needs of customers.
B. New businesses must determine who their target market is.
C. Market research identifies what your customers need and want.

### 4.2 Create the Marketing Plan
A. Primary data market research involves six steps.
B. The marketing strategy identifies how goals will be achieved.
C. A written marketing plan is a guiding document for the business.

### 4.3 Identify Your Competition
A. There are two types of competition—direct and indirect.
B. A competitive analysis finds competitors' strengths and weaknesses.
C. Businesses can maintain customer loyalty by asking for customer feedback, providing superior service, and offering incentives.

### 4.4 The Marketing Mix—Product and Price
A. A product mix is the different products and services a business sells.
B. Prices need to be high enough that revenues exceed expenses.

### 4.5 The Marketing Mix—Distribution and Promotion
A. Channels of distribution may be direct or indirect.
B. Promotion can include advertising, publicity, personal selling, and sales promotions.

## Vocabulary Builder

Choose the term that best fits the definition. Write the letter of the answer in the space provided. Some terms may not be used.

_____ 1. A system for collecting, recording, and analyzing information about customers, competitors, goods and services

_____ 2. The individuals or companies that are interested in a particular product or service and are willing and able to pay for it

_____ 3. Competition from a business that makes most of its money selling the same or similar products

_____ 4. Free promotion generated by media coverage

_____ 5. A set of processes—planning, pricing, promoting, distributing, and selling—used to satisfy the needs of customers

_____ 6. Percentage of a market owned by a business

_____ 7. Routes that products and services take from the time they are produced to the time they are consumed

_____ 8. Paid form of communication by a business about a product or service

a. advertising
b. channels of distribution
c. direct competition
d. indirect competition
e. market research
f. market share
g. marketing
h. marketing mix
i. marketing plan
j. marketing strategy
k. product mix
l. publicity
m. target market

# Review Concepts

**Point Your Browser**

www.cengage.com/
school/business/21biz

9. Why are customers so important to a business? Why is it important to listen to your customers?

_____

_____

_____

10. Describe the types of primary data market research. What is the purpose of conducting market research?

_____

_____

11. Why is it important to complete the last step of the primary market research process—evaluate the results?

_____

_____

_____

12. Why is it important to identify your direct and indirect competition?

_____

_____

13. What topics should you consider when developing your marketing plan?

_____

_____

_____

14. How do you identify your product mix?

_____

_____

15. Describe methods of setting prices.

_____

_____

_____

16. Why should established businesses advertise? Why do new businesses need to advertise?

_____

_____

_____

17. How do you choose an advertising medium?

_____

_____

18. What are the advantages and disadvantages of publicity?

_____

_____

_____

19. What is the purpose of sales promotions?

_____

_____

_____

20. Why are personal-selling skills important?

_____

_____

_____

21. What is the importance of identifying short-term goals?

_____

_____

_____

22. What are some of the ways to increase market share?

_____

_____

23. Why do you need to write a marketing plan?

_____

_____

_____

## Apply What You Learned

24. You want to start a word processing company that targets high school students who want someone else to key their term papers. Design a survey that would help you determine if there is a market for your company. Determine the best way to administer the survey. Have 30 students who are not from your class fill out the survey. Analyze the results and put them in written form.

25. You are thinking about opening a lawn-service business. Working with a small group of classmates, develop a customer profile. Make a list of competitors for the lawn-service business. Prepare a competitive analysis and create a strategy for dealing with your competition.

26. You are a home improvement contractor. What role will channels of distribution play in your business? Detail the pricing method you will use. Which form of promotion will work best for you? Outline your plans in a one-page report.

# Make Academic Connections

27. **Math** You own a photography shop. The wholesale price of a digital camera is $225. You use cost-based pricing and mark up the price by 35 percent. How much will you charge for the digital camera? There is another photography store in your town that sells a similar camera for less money. Should you lower your price? Why or why not?

_____

_____

28. **Math** You have two digital cameras left from last year's line and would like to sell them quickly. Their retail price is $325. You decide to mark them down 30 percent. What will the markdown price be?

_____

_____

29. **Research** Use the Internet to find the names of four companies that might be able to help you conduct market research. Record information such as how long the company has been in business and what kinds of market research the business does. Record your findings and compare them with the findings of other students.

30. **Research** You are opening a home entertainment store. Locate distributors, wholesalers, and manufacturers for one of your products. Choose three brands of one item and contact the distributor to obtain information about pricing and delivery. What is the wholesale price of each product? Find the same product in a local store. What is the retail price? Calculate the markup percentage.

31. **Communication** You are opening a fitness center. Because you have limited financial resources, you need to use your promotion budget carefully. Write a press release to send to the local newspapers and radio and television stations. You are also buying time on a local radio station. Write the commercial that will air on the radio. List some publicity activities that could be used to promote your business.

# Ethical Dilemma

32. You offer a math tutoring service for students at the elementary and middle schools in your neighborhood. You usually charge $15 per hour. You recently received a message from the mother of a fifth grader inquiring about your services and pricing. She was referred by the mother of another student you tutor. You would like to charge her more than $15 per hour because you know that her family is wealthy. What would you do? Is it fair for you to raise your price because you know the family has more money? What problems do you think you might experience if you charge customers different prices? What circumstances, if any, would justify charging your customers different prices?

# CHAPTER 5

# Human Resource Management

**5.1** Hire Employees

**5.2** Create a Compensation Package

**5.3** Manage Your Staff

## Careers for Entrepreneurs

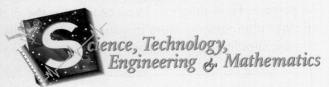

### TREMONT ELECTRIC, LLC

Tired of needing to charge his Walkman while hiking in the mountains, Aaron Lemieux wondered why his own energy could not be used to charge his Walkman. So, in 2006, Aaron left his job as a consultant to a Fortune 100 company, turned his family's basement into a laboratory, and began working full time on the nPower™ Personal Energy Generator (PEG).

Over the next two years, Aaron established Tremont Electric, LLC and assembled a team to commercialize the nPower technology. The company launched prototypes at the 2009 Consumer Electronics Show in Las Vegas and began selling online and through retail outlets across the United States in July 2009.

Today, Tremont Electric is committed to using the least amount of resources necessary to manufacture, market, and distribute products; educating employees, shareholders, and customers regarding environmental concerns and efforts; and measuring the benefits of utilizing nPower technology.

### Think Critically

1. Identify uses for the nPower technology.
2. Do you think alternative energy sources are important to the future of our economy? Explain your answer.

# PROJECT | Hiring for Your Business

## Project Objectives
- Analyze hiring needs for your business
- Develop a compensation package for employees
- Prepare a company handbook, training manual, and motivation plan for your employees

©Charlene Bayerle, 2009/ Used under license from Shutterstock.com

## Getting Started

Read the Project Process below. Make a list of any materials you will need.
- Think about the business idea you came up with in Chapter 1. If you were to open this business, what would you need to hire employees to do?
- What should you include in a handbook and training plan for new hires?

## Project Process

**5.1** Make a list of at least five jobs to be filled at your business. Is each job full-time, part-time, or occasional work? Write a detailed description and a classified ad for each job. What characteristics and qualifications are you seeking? Write interview questions.

**5.2** For each position, outline the wages, salary, and non-salary benefits. Explain why you have structured the compensation package in this way.

**5.3** Prepare a handbook of policies for vacations, holidays, hours, dress, and so on. Write a procedure for employee evaluation. Create a performance appraisal form. Determine ways to motivate your employees. How will you train new and existing employees?

## Chapter Review

**Project Wrap-up** Using a word processing program, key all the information that you have prepared in this project in an attractive format. Add this to the business plan you started in Chapter 2.

©Rob Marmion, 2009/ Used under license from Shutterstock.com

**JUMP START**

Kim had been very busy getting her paralegal service business up and running and had decided that it was time to hire some help. Richard ran a restaurant in the same town and had been hiring employees for years. Kim knew he could give her some good advice. Richard explained that it is important for Kim to decide exactly what she needs an employee to do before she hires someone. He suggested that Kim make a list of the responsibilities and then write a job description. Richard then explained the various ways Kim could recruit employees by using the job description she created. Why do you think a job description is so important?

### GOALS

Determine the positions your business needs

Describe the hiring process

Identify alternatives to hiring permanent staff

### KEY TERMS

**job description,** p. 129

**job analysis,** p. 129

**organizational structure,** p. 129

**recruit,** p. 130

## Identify a Need for Employees

To succeed, you probably will need to hire employees. The people who work for you are your *human resources*. Employees can help your business run efficiently. Good employees will help you attract customers and increase sales. But how do you know what kinds of employees you need? And how do you go about getting them? To find out your hiring needs, ask these questions.

- What kind of employees do I need?
- What skills am I missing?
- What skills do I need daily?
- What skills do I need occasionally?

List all the duties in your business. Then identify how much time is needed to perform each duty. Your list should help you identify whether you need part-time, full-time, or temporary workers. You can also determine if you need managers or assistants and how many employees you need.

## Write Job Descriptions

A *job* is a collection of tasks and duties that an employee is responsible for completing. A *task* is a specific work activity that is performed, such as answering e-mail or paying bills. Many positions include a variety of tasks that are sometimes referred to as *functions*. A job description is a written statement listing the tasks and responsibilities of a position. Job descriptions also indicate to whom the position reports, educational and professional experience required, and salary range. Job descriptions are written after conducting a job analysis, which is the process of determining the tasks and sequence of tasks necessary to perform a job.

A detailed job description makes clear the job responsibilities. If a receptionist objects to ordering supplies, his employer can remind him that this task is included in his job description. The tasks and responsibilities outlined in the job description also can be used to measure how well an employee performs a job and help determine how much money to offer applicants.

### SAMPLE JOB DESCRIPTION

**Title:** Account Executive

**Tasks and responsibilities:** Plans, coordinates, and directs advertising campaigns for clients of advertising agency. Coordinates budget and activities of workers engaged in marketing research, writing copy, laying out artwork, purchasing media time and space, developing special displays and promotional items, and performing other media-production activities.

**Qualifications:** College degree with courses in marketing, leadership, communication, business, and advertising; sales experience; excellent interpersonal and written communication skills; and ability to work independently.

**Reports to:** Marketing Manager

**Salary:** $30,000 to $50,000, based on experience.

## Create an Organizational Structure

Once your company has several employees, you will need an organizational structure. An organizational structure shows how the various jobs relate to one another. Many businesses use a chart, such as the one shown below, to represent the organizational structure. The chart shows who reports to whom, or the *chain of command*, in the company. In some small businesses, all employees may report directly to the company owner. In larger companies, lower-level employees usually report to a supervisor. This structure ensures that the owner is not called upon to deal with relatively unimportant issues.

| ORGANIZATIONAL CHART, NORTHCLIFFE PUBLISHING | | | |
|---|---|---|---|
| Sandra Wilson, President | | | |
| Robert Gotting, Vice President | | | |
| **Production** | **Marketing** | **Design** | **Editorial** |
| **Department Head** Rose Silver | **Department Head** Martine Landy | **Department Head** Stella Jackson | **Department Head** Orlando Smythe |
| **Project Managers** Cindy Williams Stephen Ortiz | **Associates** Heidi Berger Ross Wingate | **Designers** Monroe Ross Maura O'Donnell | **Editors** Nancy Peters Paul Whitney |
| **Assistant** Rita Woo | **Assistant** Anne Husayn | **Assistant** Andrew Roberts | **Assistant** Alan Berg |

## The Hiring Process

Once you have determined that there is a need to hire employees for your company, the next steps are to recruit, interview, and select employees.

### Recruit Employees

To **recruit** is to look for people to hire and attract them to your business. You can recruit employees in a variety of ways.

**Classified Advertising** A *want ad* is a type of classified ad that announces a job opening at a company. It can be an effective way to recruit employees. A want ad should briefly describe the position and tell the educational requirements and/or experience required. It should also identify any special job requirements, such as willingness to travel or to work evenings.

**Online Career and Employment Sites** Many people now use the Internet to look for a job, so many employers are advertising with online career and employment sites. Most online employment services allow you to post a job and then search the resumes that are sent in response to the posting. Some online employment services have a database of resumes that you can review when you are looking for someone to fill a specific job.

**Employment Agencies** These agencies find employees for businesses and other institutions. They try to match people looking for jobs with businesses looking for employees. Employment agencies charge businesses a fee when they are successful.

**College Placement Centers** Most colleges and universities operate job placement centers. These offices collect information on career and employment opportunities, which they make available to their students and graduates. Generally, no fee is charged for using a college placement center. If college students or graduates might be suitable for your business, contact local colleges and universities and ask them what you need to do to have your business listed with their placement center.

**Other Ways of Recruiting Employees** One of the best ways entrepreneurs find employees is by acting on referrals from friends, acquaintances, or employees. You can also try to recruit employees by putting a help wanted sign in your store window, but be sure you have time to deal with the many people who may stop to inquire about the position. If your company already has employees, the ideal candidate for a job you need to fill might already be working for you in another position.

## Interview Job Applicants

The job interview gives you the opportunity to determine if prospective employees would improve your ability to meet customer needs. Making the most of the job interview is as important for you as it is for the job candidate. To ensure that you use your time effectively, follow these basic rules.

1. **Screen Candidates.** The first stage in the interviewing process is to screen candidates to remove the people who are not right for the job. This allows you to concentrate on looking at the most qualified candidates.

2. **Be prepared.** Make a list of open-ended questions to ask. Review the job candidate's resume and application before the interview begins.

3. **Be courteous.** Do not be late for the interview. Avoid taking phone calls during the interview. Try to put job candidates at ease by offering them something to drink. Make them feel welcome in your office.

4. **Avoid dominating the interview.** Remember that the interview is your opportunity to get to know the job candidate. To do so, be sure to allow the applicant plenty of time to speak.

5. **Take notes.** Throughout the interview, jot down your impressions of the candidate as well as any interesting information he or she reveals.

©Fred Sweet, 2009/ Used under license from Shutterstock.com

6. **Look for warnings that the person may not be a good worker.** These include frequent job changes, unexplained gaps in employment, and critical comments about previous employers.

7. **Don't make snap judgments about a candidate.** Don't rule out someone until the interview is over.

Why should you take notes when interviewing job candidates?

8. **Remain pleasant and positive throughout the interview.** At the end of the interview, thank the candidate for coming and let him or her know when you plan to make a decision.

9. **Write a summary of your impressions of the candidate.** You should do this right after the interview while your thoughts are fresh. Put this document in the candidate's file.

### SAMPLE INTERVIEW QUESTIONS

1. What interests you about the job?
2. How can your skills and experience benefit the company?
3. What are your career plans? How does this job fit in with those plans?
4. What other positions have you held? What did you like and dislike about those positions?
5. What were your achievements at your previous job?
6. Why did you leave your last job?
7. How do you think your education has prepared you for this job?
8. What kinds of work do you enjoy most? What makes a job enjoyable for you?
9. Describe a situation where you had to manage conflicting priorities.

©Andresr, 2009/ Used under license from Shutterstock.com

Why is it important to check a job candidate's references?

## Hire Employees

Once you have two or three very qualified candidates, you need to check references. With the permission of the applicant, call his or her most recent employers to make sure he or she held the positions on the resume. Ask previous employers what they can tell you about the person's work performance and people skills.

When you have decided to make a job offer, contact the person by phone. Let the person know you were impressed with his or her credentials. Be sure to emphasize how much you would like the person to join your company. Clearly state the starting salary, benefits, and terms of employment. If the first applicant declines your offer, extend the offer to your second choice and then your third choice, if necessary.

Once a candidate accepts your offer, contact all the other candidates. Thank them for interviewing with your business, and politely let them know that you have given the job to another applicant.

## CheckPOINT

What steps are involved in hiring employees?

_____

_____

# Alternatives to Adding Staff

Adding employees to your payroll is costly. Paying wages or salaries to employees may strain your finances. It also takes time and money to recruit staff. For these reasons, you may want to consider alternatives to permanent staff.

## Freelancers or Interns

*Freelancers* are people who provide services to businesses on an hourly basis or by the job. Business owners use freelancers when they need a job done but do not require a permanent full- or part-time employee. Examples of freelancers include bookkeepers, accountants, lawyers, graphic designers, editors, window display artists, and advertising copywriters.

*Interns* are students who will work for little or no pay in order to gain experience in a particular field. To find out if interns are available in your community, contact local colleges and high schools. If you hire an intern, you may have to work with the school's intern coordinator to ensure certain program requirements are fulfilled.

## Temporary Workers

Businesses that need more workers or workers with special skills often use temporary workers. Some temporary workers are seasonal employees. Others are substitutes for employees who are sick or on a leave of absence. Temporary workers also can be used for long periods of time as an alternative to a full-time worker.

Temporary employment agencies provide trained temporary workers to various kinds of businesses. Businesses that use temporary agencies pay the worker's salary plus a fee to the agency. The agency manages the worker's salary and benefits.

Northcliffe Publishing has just published a book that has become a top seller. The volume of orders has gone up so quickly that the regular employees cannot get the orders filled fast enough. Robert Gotting, vice president, is trying to decide whether or not he should hire a permanent employee to help handle the increased workload. He looks at all the costs involved in hiring a new permanent employee and decides that the company would be better off hiring a temporary employee through an agency to work in order fulfillment. If the need for another employee continues, he might decide to make the position permanent at a later time.

## CheckPOINT

What are some alternatives to hiring employees?

_____

_____

# Think Critically

1. Why is it important for a company to have an organizational structure that allows the owner to focus on long-term issues?

_____

_____

_____

_____

2. List some advantages of using an employment agency.

_____

_____

_____

_____

3. Why do you need to check a job applicant's references?

_____

_____

_____

_____

4. What would be some disadvantages of hiring freelancers and temporary workers?

_____

_____

_____

_____

# Make Academic Connections

5. **Communication** Evan Goulet opened a motorcycle repair shop several years ago. He has decided to hire two mechanics and a receptionist. Write an ad to be placed in your local newspaper for each of the new positions.

6. **Management** Create an organizational structure for a 30-person local package delivery service. First, determine all the types of employees the business would have. Then create the chart based on your decisions.

7. **Research** Create a resource guide containing online career and employment websites, employment agencies, and college placement centers that could be used to help meet staffing needs for your business.

### JUMP START

After writing job descriptions and placing ads in the local newspaper, Kim now has candidates lined up for interviews. She went back to Richard for more advice. Richard suggested that she make a list of questions to ask all applicants. Kim realized that the information gathered during the interview, along with the applicants' references and application forms, would help her decide whom to hire. Richard reminded her that the applicants would probably have questions for her as well—such as how much she was going to pay. Kim had not yet decided on pay rates. Richard explained the various ways of compensating employees, including benefits. Kim knew she had some homework to do before her first interview. Why do you think the salary and benefits Kim offers will be so important?

©Scott Rothstein-2009/Used under license from Shutterstock.com

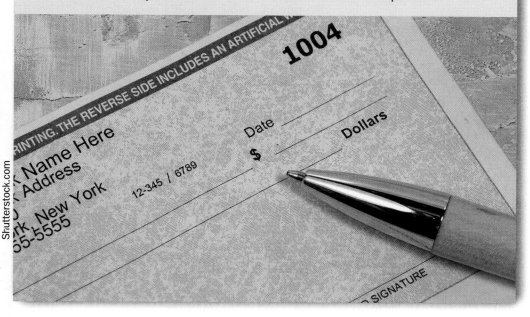

**GOALS**

Determine how to pay employees

Describe the benefits portion of a compensation package

**KEY TERMS**

wages, p. 135

salaries, p. 135

bonus, p. 135

profit sharing, p. 136

commission, p. 136

## Types of Pay

As an entrepreneur with paid employees, you will need to create a compensation package. The package should include payment and may provide a variety of benefits.

**Wages** are payments for labor or services that are made on an hourly, daily, or per-unit basis. The paycheck for a person earning a wage will vary depending on how many hours are worked or how many units are manufactured. **Salaries** are fixed payments for labor or services stated on an annual basis. Regardless of the number of hours salaried employees work, the amount of money they are paid does not vary.

Employees may also receive a **bonus**, which is a financial reward made in addition to a regular wage or salary. Bonuses usually depend on reaching an

**TEAMWORK**

In small groups, make a list of jobs that are commonly paid by a wage, a salary, and a commission. Discuss why you think the different methods are used for each job.

©Jason Stitt, 2009/ Used under license from Shutterstock.com

What type of compensation plan would you prefer? Why?

established goal. **Profit sharing** is another compensation arrangement in which employees are paid a portion of the company's profits. Some employees are paid a **commission**, which is a percentage of a sale paid to a salesperson. A commission-based salary varies from month to month, depending on sales. Those receiving this type of salary may be paid using a commission-only plan or a combination plan, which combines a commission with a salary or hourly wage.

In most markets, wages and salaries are competitively determined. This means that an employer who offers much less than the going wage or salary rate is not likely to find qualified workers.

To offer competitive wages or salaries, you will have to find out how much similar businesses in your area are paying their employees. You should also find out what people are earning in jobs with similar qualifications. Once you know what the going wage or salary is, you will have to decide whether you want to offer more than, less than, or about the same as other businesses. Offering more than other businesses will attract the best employees.

## Business Math Connection

Lyn Kovacs sold $490,000 worth of electronic devices last year. If she receives a 10 percent commission, what is her annual commission? If she is paid on a combination plan with a $20,000 salary plus a 5 percent commission, what is her annual pay? Does she make more on the commission-only plan or on the combination plan?

**SOLUTION**
Use the following formula to calculate a commission.

Amount sold × Percent of commission = Amount of commission
$490,000 × 0.10 = $49,000

On a commission-only plan, Lyn's annual pay is $49,000.

For the combination plan, first calculate the amount of commission.

$490,000 × 0.05 = $24,500   Amount of commission

Then, add the base wages or salary and the amount of commission to calculate the total pay.

Base salary + Amount of commission = Total pay
$20,000 + $24,500 = $44,500

On the combination plan, Lyn's annual pay is $44,500. She would make more on the commission-only plan.

# Benefits

Benefits are employment rewards for service in addition to pay. They include paid days off from work, various kinds of insurance, and retirement plans.

## Paid Leave

Almost all employers offer paid vacation and sick leave. Both kinds of leave represent costs to employers because employees are paid while they are not working. Be aware that some employees may abuse paid sick leave. Someone in your business should keep a record of the paid leave employees take.

**Vacation** Businesses handle vacation in various ways. Many offer one or two weeks of paid vacation a year to new employees. Employees usually gain more vacation time the longer they work at a business. Some businesses let employees carry vacation days from year to year while others require employees to use their vacation time in one year.

**Sick Leave** Sometimes your employees will not be able to make it into work because of illness. The number of days of sick leave provided varies from business to business. Some businesses offer only five sick days a year. Others allow employees unlimited sick leave. You will have to develop a sick leave policy that is fair to your employees but not excessively costly to you.

## Insurance

Most large businesses offer insurance as a benefit. Because of high costs, this kind of benefit is less common among small businesses, although many do provide such coverage. When businesses do offer insurance benefits, employees often have to pay a portion of the cost. Usually, all full-time employees are eligible for this benefit. You can decide to offer these benefits to part-time employees as well.

**Health Benefits** Business owners with many employees may be able to purchase discounted group medical insurance or enroll employees in a health maintenance organization (HMO). You can offer either or both options to your employees as a benefit of working for your business. People with medical insurance or HMO coverage pay a monthly fee whether or not they are sick. In return, the insurance company or HMO agrees to cover most of their medical bills.

## SOCIAL SECURITY IN GREECE

In the United States, employers and employees both make contributions to the Social Security Administration to provide coverage for benefits for workers upon retirement and medical insurance through Medicare. In Greece, the largest social security organization is IKA. The cost of IKA is 350 euros (approximately $500 U.S.) every two months, which is split 50-50 by the employer and employee. IKA covers employees in Greece or abroad for a Greek-based employer. IKA also covers workers who offer full-time or part-time labor on commissioned work agreements and are not insured with any other insurance agency. The main role of social security in Greece is to offer free or low-cost insurance coverage to its members for medical examinations and treatments at IKA laboratories. IKA also provides hospitalization and prescription drug coverage as well as dental care.

### Think Critically

Would you consider participation in this system to be an employee benefit? Why or why not?

**Other Kinds of Insurance** Some businesses also offer other kinds of insurance. *Dental insurance* covers the cost of dental and orthodontic expenses. *Life insurance* is intended to provide financial support for families after the income earner dies. *Accidental insurance* provides financial support to people who are in accidents.

### Retirement Plans

Some businesses help employees save for retirement by offering 401(k) plans. Employees that participate in 401(k) plans have a percentage of their earned income withheld by the employer to be deposited into a professionally managed investment account. Some employers will match employee's 401(k) contributions as much as 50 cents per dollar invested. The funds will continue to grow tax-free until they are withdrawn by the retiree upon reaching retirement age. Pension plans are another type of employer-sponsored retirement savings plan, but they are not as common because they are more costly to a company.

## CheckPOINT

List three types of non-salary benefits a business might offer.

_____

_____

# Think Critically

1. Why might a combination plan salary be attractive to an employee?

_____

_____

_____

_____

_____

2. Using examples, explain why employees' personal lives might influence their desire for different types of benefits.

_____

_____

_____

_____

# Make Academic Connections

3. **Math**  You have received two job offers for similar sales positions. Company A pays a salary of $21,000 per year. Company B offers a combination plan of $12,000 per year plus a commission of 15 percent of sales. You are told that the average first-year salesperson at Company B has about $90,000 in total annual sales. Which job will you choose and why?

_____

_____

_____

4. **Research**  Look in a newspaper or on the Internet for help wanted job descriptions that contain benefits. In a paragraph, briefly describe the benefits that appeal to you and explain why.

5. **Communication**  Interview five adults you know who have full-time or part-time jobs. Ask them if they receive wages, salary, or a commission. Ask what types of benefits they receive. Ask which of these benefits is most important to them and why. Put your findings in a chart and share with your class.

6. **Problem Solving**  Barry Sandler, owner of Sandler's Custom Computers, has decided to change the way sales associates are paid. They are currently paid a salary. Barry gathers the sales team together to get their suggestions. As a class, decide on a new compensation method for the company. Your teacher will role-play Barry Sandler.

### GOALS

Recognize how to lead your employees by enforcing policies and offering training

Determine how to motivate your employees

Discuss how to evaluate your employees

### KEY TERMS

delegate, p. 143

performance appraisal, p. 144

 **JUMP START**

Kim hired her first employee, Justin, and she was anxiously awaiting his first day of work. She realized it would be very important for her to explain to Justin exactly what she needed him to do as well as her expectations regarding matters like attendance, dress, and breaks. To welcome Justin to the company, she decided to make a booklet explaining all of the company's policies. Kim realized that managing an employee required planning. In order for Justin to do a good job, she would have to be a good manager. What kinds of things do you think Kim should do to be a good manager?

©Dmitry Yashkin, 2009/ Used under license from Shutterstock.com

## Lead Your Employees

Once you have people working for you, you will become a manager. This means that you will no longer focus all of your efforts on doing your own job. Much of your time will be spent managing other people. As a manager, you will have to exhibit leadership and motivate your employees.

### Desirable Leadership Qualities

To manage your staff effectively, you will need to develop good leadership qualities. Good leadership qualities will help you create a workforce that is dedicated to meeting customer needs and increasing sales.

There are many personal characteristics that can help you be a good leader. Desirable leadership qualities include

- Judgment—making decisions carefully and objectively
- Honesty—applying ethics in your decisions and treatment of others
- Consistency—being predictable and emotionally even
- Enthusiasm—generating enthusiasm in others
- Cooperation—working well with others
- Communications—listening, speaking, and writing effectively
- Dependability—following through on commitments
- Understanding—respecting feelings and needs of people

Developing these qualities has helped Adam Stevenson create a team of dedicated employees at the busy tool rental shop he owns. Every month Adam posts the work schedule for the following month. He makes sure to assign the unpopular night and weekend shifts evenly among all his employees. Adam encourages employees who want to make schedule changes to discuss their needs with him. He tries to accommodate all reasonable requests. Adam urges all employees to come to him with suggestions for improving service. He also praises employees who have good ideas, and he lets others know of their contributions.

## Enforce Employee Policies

As the owner of your own business, you will establish policies concerning vacations, holidays, hours, acceptable dress, and other issues affecting your workers. You will need to make sure that all of your employees are familiar with these policies. This may mean gently reminding employees if they fail to follow them.

Many companies communicate policies to staff by creating an employee handbook. These handbooks can be just a few pages long or they can fill a small binder, depending on the size of your company and the number of policies.

## Train Your Employees

Well-trained employees perform their jobs well. They know what is expected of them, so they have higher morale and are less likely to quit. Poorly trained employees do not perform well. They become frustrated by lack of training and look for new jobs.

You will need to develop a training program for your new employees. This program should begin as soon as they are hired. Training should not end when the employee learns how things are done. Continuous improvement of employees through the use of ongoing training will help your business.

### NETBookmark

Many businesses with employees benefit from having an employee handbook. By formally writing down policies and providing clear guidelines, entrepreneurs spend less time answering questions and explaining company rules and regulations. But businesses sometimes make mistakes when they create their employee handbooks. Access www.cengage.com/school/business/21biz and click on the link for Chapter 5. Read the article and then answer: Which of the mistakes described do you think is potentially the riskiest for a business? Why? How often should an employee handbook be updated?

**www.cengage.com/school/business/21biz**

There are techniques for providing training to employees. You may use different techniques for different job responsibilities.

1. **On-the-job training** Employees learn new responsibilities by actually performing them at their place of business.

2. **Coaching** Employees receive feedback and instruction from their manager on a constant basis.

3. **Mentoring** One employee teams up with another more experienced employee to learn a job.

4. **Conferences and seminars** Employees attend meetings to learn new techniques or duties from an expert in the field.

After training, you need to make sure employees are using that training and that the training has been effective. After employees have had a chance to apply the new processes or procedures to their job, you may need to have a follow-up meeting to determine how well things are going and to address any issues that have arisen since the training.

Your employees also should be thoroughly trained in safety issues. They should know how to operate equipment safely or wear any necessary protective gear. Employees should be briefed on emergency plans for fires, tornadoes, and other disasters. You should also map evacuation routes on your floor plan and post these throughout your building.

## CheckPOINT

Why is it important to have employee policies and a training program?

_____

_____

# Motivate Your Employees

To get the most out of your employees, you will have to motivate them. You can do so in several ways.

1. **Pay them well.** When employees feel they are compensated well, they will be happier. They will perform to the best of their ability.

2. **Treat them fairly.** Everyone wants to be treated well. Be sure to treat everyone the same.

3. **Recognize them for the work they do.** Offer public recognition of good work. Praise employees frequently.

4. **Give them adequate responsibility.** Employees who are allowed to make decisions often work harder.

How can you motivate your employees to perform well?

They take pride in the fact that their work can make a difference.

## Delegate Responsibility

Many entrepreneurs have difficulty delegating responsibility. To **delegate** is to let other people share workloads and responsibilities. Employees who are given more responsibility are better motivated and contribute more to the company. Delegating responsibility to them allows you to make the most of their talents.

Delegating allows you to focus on important items, such as expanding into new markets or offering new products. Paperwork and duties that someone else can perform will not bog you down.

Finally, delegating responsibility is essential if a company is to grow. When your business is small, you may be able to handle all areas of its management. If the company is to expand, though, you will have to let managers and other employees take on more and more responsibility.

## Listen to Employees

Some entrepreneurs fail to listen to their employees. In doing so, they miss out on an opportunity to take advantage of valuable resources that can help them increase profits.

The people who work for you are very familiar with your business and may be able to offer fresh ideas. Listening to new points of view may help you come up with new, creative solutions. If you value the opinions of your employees, they will feel they are a valuable asset to your company. This means they will most likely be motivated to do a good job for you.

**TEAMWORK**

In small groups, brainstorm a list of personal qualities that effective team members should possess.

## Work as a Team

In many activities, working together as a team determines whether or not an effort is successful. A ball club cannot win if its players do not work together as a team. Astronauts working on the space station cannot complete their mission if crew members do not work together.

Teamwork is important in many businesses. Employees who work as a team are usually very committed. They are more likely to work harder and to come up with creative ideas for increasing profits.

Creating an atmosphere in which employees feel part of a team is a big challenge. You should try to create an atmosphere in which all of your employees work toward a common goal. Respecting, communicating with, and getting along with other team members is also important.

As a business owner, it will be up to you to provide the leadership and motivation that will allow your employees to work together as a team. To be an effective team leader you will need to

- Establish trust among team members and gain their trust
- Make sure that all team members understand the goals you have set
- Encourage team members to be creative and innovative
- Make team members feel like partners in your business
- Help team members learn from their mistakes
- Build the team's commitment to achieving the goals you have set

---

## CheckPOINT

How can working as a team help your business succeed?

_____

_____

---

# Evaluate Your Employees

At least once a year you need to evaluate how well employees are doing their jobs. Evaluating performance will help you determine whether an employee should be given a raise. It also will help you identify outstanding employees who should be promoted and problem employees who should be dismissed.

## Create an Evaluation Procedure

Most businesses perform an annual employee **performance appraisal**, which is a management control tool that helps determine whether the objectives for a particular job are being met. The original job description should be used when evaluating how well an employee has performed his or her job. If the employee has fulfilled all of his or her job responsibilities, that employee should receive a wage or salary increase.

You should record the review on an appraisal form, such as the one shown below. The employee's name and job title should be listed, as well as the manager's name, the date range the evaluation covers, job responsibilities and attributes, comments, goals for the next year, and areas for improvement. A ranking method can be used to mark how well the employee has performed.

## PERFORMANCE APPRAISAL

DATE: January 21, 20—
NAME: Daniel Tisdale
JOB TITLE: Marketing Director

Reports To: Laureen Stiles
Review Period: 1/1 to 12/31

| ATTRIBUTE | WELL ABOVE STANDARD | ABOVE STANDARD | STANDARD | BELOW STANDARD | FAR BELOW STANDARD |
|---|---|---|---|---|---|
| Quantity of work | | ✓ | | | |
| Knowledge of work | | ✓ | | | |
| Ability to organize | | | ✓ | | |
| Meets deadlines | | | ✓ | | |
| Dependability | | | ✓ | | |
| Judgment | | | ✓ | | |
| Initiative | ✓ | | | | |
| Communication | | | | ✓ | |
| Manages others well | | | ✓ | | |
| Teamwork | | | ✓ | | |

**COMMENTS:** You have done an outstanding job of increasing sales. Your hard work, dependability, and initiative are very much appreciated.

**AREAS FOR IMPROVEMENT:**

1. Increase technical knowledge so that quality of work matches quantity of work.
2. Improve written communication skills by enrolling in a business writing course.
3. Improve management skills, in particular by delegating more responsibility to your marketing assistants.
4. Increase ability to participate as part of team.

**GOALS FOR COMING YEAR:**

1. Increase store sales 12 percent.
2. Oversee completion of company website.
3. Generate online sales of $75,000.

Employee: Daniel Tisdale

Manager: Laureen Stiles

_Daniel Tisdale_

_Laureen Stiles_

How can performance appraisals benefit the employer and employee?

Reviews in which you let employees know how they have performed during the year should be conducted face to face. A written summary of the review should be kept in your general employee file.

## Promote Employees

Promoting good employees will help ensure that they remain interested in working for your business. Employees often compete with one another, so promoting one employee over another may cause problems. Be sure that you make all decisions fairly. Base your decision on solid reasons, such as volume of sales and quality of customer service.

## Dismiss Employees

Some employees may not work out. In fact, they may end up hurting your business. How will you handle such situations? As soon as you notice an employee not performing well, discuss the situation with him or her. If performance does not improve, issue a written warning. If there is still no improvement, you will need to dismiss that employee.

Once you decide to dismiss an employee, do so immediately. Meet with the employee privately and explain why you are letting him or her go. Ask him to leave the workplace the same day. Record the date of the termination and the reason for termination in the employee's file.

## CheckPOINT

Why should you evaluate the people who work for you?

_____

_____

# Think Critically

1. List five desirable characteristics of leadership.

_____

_____

_____

2. What are the different job training techniques?

_____

_____

3. What are four ways to motivate your employees?

_____

_____

4. Why do you think it is difficult for many entrepreneurs to delegate?

_____

_____

_____

5. How is a work team similar to a sports team? How is it different?

_____

_____

_____

6. Why do you think it is important to keep a written summary of a performance evaluation?

_____

_____

_____

# Make Academic Connections

7. **Communication** With a partner, role-play an evaluation for an employee who deserves a promotion. Make up the employer and job. Use the performance appraisal form in this lesson and revise the attributes as needed to fit the job. Summarize the meeting in writing.

8. **Problem Solving** You own a clothing store and currently employ two sales assistants. You have just hired a new sales assistant. Develop a training program for your new employee so she will learn all aspects of the business, including operating the cash register, assisting customers, and opening and closing the store.

## Chapter Summary

**5.1** **Hire Employees**

A. To succeed as an entrepreneur, you will need to hire employees. You should write job descriptions that list the specific responsibilities of each job. You should also create an organizational structure that shows how the different jobs in your company relate to each other.

B. You can use a variety of methods to recruit employees. When hiring employees, you will first need to screen applicants and then interview those who seem good for the job. Check the references of your final candidates and then offer the position to the most qualified person.

C. In addition to hiring permanent employees, you can also hire freelancers, interns, or temporary workers.

**5.2** **Create a Compensation Package**

A. Determine the wages, salaries, or commissions you will give your employees. Be sure to pay competitively.

B. You might also offer benefits, including paid leave, insurance plans, and retirement plans.

**5.3** **Manage Your Staff**

A. Having good leadership qualities, enforcing policies, and offering training will help you manage your staff effectively.

B. Motivate your employees to get the most out of them. You can motivate your employees by treating them fairly and listening to them.

C. Create a procedure for evaluating employees. Outstanding employees should be promoted, and problem employees should be dismissed.

## Vocabulary Builder

Choose the term that best fits the definition. Write the letter of the answer in the space provided. Some terms may not be used.

_____ 1. To look for people to hire

_____ 2. Management control tool that helps determine whether the objectives for a particular job are being met

_____ 3. Plan showing how the various jobs in a company relate to one another

_____ 4. Written statement listing job tasks and responsibilities

_____ 5. Process of determining the tasks necessary to perform a job

_____ 6. Fixed payments for labor or services stated on an annual basis

_____ 7. Payments for labor or services that are made on an hourly, daily, or per-unit basis

_____ 8. Percentage of a sale paid to a salesperson

_____ 9. To let other people share workloads and responsibilities

_____10. Financial reward in addition to a regular wage or salary

a. bonus

b. commission

c. delegate

d. job analysis

e. job description

f. organizational structure

g. performance appraisal

h. profit sharing

i. recruit

j. salaries

k. wages

# Review Concepts

**11.** Why is it important to write a detailed job description?

_____

_____

_____

**12.** Why is it important to create an organizational structure?

_____

_____

_____

**13.** What type of information should a want ad contain?

_____

_____

_____

**14.** What are some of the characteristics of a desirable employee?

_____

_____

_____

_____

**15.** List the things you should do while interviewing a candidate.

_____

_____

_____

_____

**16.** Why might you consider alternatives to hiring permanent employees?

_____

_____

_____

**17.** How are wages and salaries determined in most markets?

_____

_____

**18.** Name the five different types of pay.

_____

_____

_____

**19.** What are some of the most common benefits offered to employees?

_____

_____

_____

**20.** Why are good leadership qualities necessary to manage a staff?

_____

_____

_____

_____

21. Why is it important to give employees adequate responsibility?

_____

_____

22. What are the methods for training employees?

_____

_____

23. Why is teamwork important in many businesses?

_____

_____

24. Why do you need to evaluate your employees?

_____

_____

## Apply What You Learned

25. You have decided to hire three people to help in your custom drapery business: a receptionist, an interior designer (salesperson), and a tailor. What qualifications and skills must each of these employees possess? Write a job description for each position. For each job, establish a compensation package. Did you structure the compensation differently for each employee? How will you recruit these employees? Write a list of interview questions that you will ask each candidate.

26. Each of the employees in your drapery business has completed one year of service. Complete a performance appraisal form for each employee. What types of goals did you set for each employee? How will you decide if your employees are entitled to a raise or promotion?

27. To pay competitively, employers must know what similar businesses pay their employees. What are some of the ways to find out compensation levels at similar businesses? How do you decide whether you want to offer more than, less than, or the same compensation as other businesses?

_____

_____

_____

28. Good leadership qualities are essential to manage effectively. Are good leadership qualities something that can be learned, or are you born with them? Why do you think so?

_____

_____

_____

_____

# Make Academic Connections

**29. Math**  Jayne Smith sells vacuum cleaners and is compensated under a combination plan. She earns $9.25 per hour plus 15 percent of whatever she sells. Last month, Jayne worked 160 hours and sold 9 vacuum cleaners. Five of the vacuum cleaners were top-of-the-line models with a price of $1,100 each. The remaining vacuum cleaners were $450 each. What was Jayne's compensation last month?

_____

_____

_____

**30. Research**  Compare three advertisements for the same type of job. What are the job titles? What are the qualifications for each? What is the compensation and how is it structured? Using the Internet, find out what the average pay is for this position. Organize the information you gather into a table or spreadsheet.

**31. Problem Solving**  One of your employees is upset that another employee received a promotion. The first employee thinks she deserved the promotion because she has been with the company longer. How will you deal with the situation?

_____

_____

_____

_____

# Ethical Dilemma

**32.**  You want to hire a new sales assistant for your company. You checked with the local college placement office, and it sent several qualified applicants for an interview. You are really impressed with one of the candidates, and you want to hire him for the position. Before making the job offer, you decide to check the Internet to see if the candidate has a personal web page that might provide you with more information regarding his background and interests. By performing an Internet search, you quickly find his personal web page. You are shocked at some of the pictures he has posted and at some of the activities in which he has participated. What would you do? Would you hire him anyway or would this change your impression of him?

_____

_____

_____

_____

# Finance, Protect, and Insure Your Business

## Careers for Entrepreneurs

*Business Management & Administration*

### LIFE IS GOOD

Perhaps you own a "Life is good" shirt or some other item with Jake's smiley-face stick figure on it. Bert and John Jacobs, founders of the casual clothing company Life is good, have found the slogan to be true and want to share that feeling with others. As demand for their product increased, they had to make decisions about how to grow their company while staying true to their belief in the simple pleasures of life.

When it came time to decide on an advertising campaign for the company, Bert and John decided to forego the traditional advertising route and instead invest the money to help those in need. Today the company works with a number of charitable organizations and holds a series of festivals each year in the New England area. Although it started out as a different way to spend marketing dollars, today, charitable work has become a major focus for the company.

### Think Critically

1. What do you think about Bert and John's decision to spend their advertising dollars doing good for the community?
2. Do you think this decision has helped their company to grow more than it would have with a conventional advertising campaign?

# PROJECT | Finance, Protect, and Insure Your Business

## Project Objectives

- Prepare financial statements for your business
- Determine how much money you will need to borrow and where to borrow the money
- Establish a security plan and determine insurance needs for your business

©Alexander Kalina, 2009/ Used under license from Shutterstock.com

## Getting Started

Read the Project Process below. Make a list of any materials you will need.

- Think about the business idea you came up with in Chapter 1. If you were to open this business, how much do you think it would cost?
- What are the types of things you would need to get the business started? How would you protect your business once it is open?

## Project Process

**6.1** Prepare a list of startup costs and the cash flow statement, income statement, balance sheet, and personal financial statement.

**6.2** Determine how much money, if any, you need to borrow to begin your business. Decide where you will obtain financing.

**6.3** Write how you will prevent employee theft, shoplifting, robberies, credit card fraud, and bad checks. Contact an insurance agent about the types of insurance you need.

## Chapter Review

**Project Wrap-up**  Using a word processing program, key all the information that you have prepared in this project. Complete the business plan you started in Chapter 2. Present your business plan to your class.

©Stephen Coburn, 2009/ Used under license from Shutterstock.com

### GOALS

Calculate your startup costs

Prepare financial statements for your business

### KEY TERMS

**startup costs,** p. 155

**operating expenses,** p. 156

**assets,** p. 158

**liabilities,** p. 158

**owner's equity,** p. 158

**depreciation,** p. 159

 **JUMP START**

Frank and Jeremy saw a need for a customized calendar business at their school. Students wanted to use their own pictures and have all the important school dates as well as dates of personal interest to them on the calendars. Frank and Jeremy researched calendar software and printing options and came up with a style that would fit in student lockers and allow them to do the needed customization. They calculated startup costs for supplies, software, a computer, a color laser printer, and laminating and binding machines. Their next step was to project their income and expenses for the upcoming year. They knew that during months when special holidays occurred, they would probably sell more calendars, and expenses would be greater. Frank and Jeremy would use their projections to compile the necessary financial statements. Why is it important for Frank and Jeremy to prepare financial statements before starting their business?

©Yuri Arcurs, 2009/ Used under license from Shutterstock.com

## Get Started with Finances

All businesses need money to survive. However, many entrepreneurs lack the money they need to start and run a business. In fact, lack of money is one of the main reasons that small businesses fail. How can entrepreneurs with solid business ideas get the financing to start and run a business? Before you can approach a lender or investor about financing your business, you will have to prepare financial statements. These statements allow potential lenders and investors to decide if your business is viable and whether the financing you are requesting is reasonable.

Before you can begin preparing financial statements, you must calculate your startup costs. **Startup costs** are the one-time-only expenses that are paid to establish a business. Common startup costs include

- Equipment and supplies, such as cash registers, computers, telephones, and fax machines
- Furniture and fixtures, such as desks and chairs
- Vehicles, including delivery trucks and other automobiles
- Remodeling, such as electrical and plumbing expenses
- Legal and accounting fees
- Licensing fees

Startup costs should be considered when you are figuring out how much money you need to start your business. Most entrepreneurs have to borrow the money needed to cover startup costs.

Felicia Walters plans to start a lighting fixture store. To help her determine how much money she will need to borrow, she calculates her startup costs. She must include her estimate of startup costs with the other documents she provides to lenders.

| STARTUP COSTS, WALTERS ELECTRIC | |
|---|---|
| **Item** | **Estimated Cost** |
| **Equipment and supplies** | |
| Computers (3 @ $1,500) | $ 4,500 |
| Modem | 175 |
| Cash registers (2 @ $1,800) | 3,600 |
| Fax machine | 400 |
| Supplies | 300 |
| **Subtotal** | **$ 8,975** |
| **Furniture and fixtures** | |
| Desks (4 @ $400) | $ 1,600 |
| Chairs (8 @ $75) | 600 |
| **Subtotal** | **$ 2,200** |
| **Vehicles** | |
| Delivery truck | $10,000 |
| Automobile | 8,000 |
| **Subtotal** | **$18,000** |
| **Remodeling** | |
| Drywall replacement | $ 1,000 |
| Electrical work | 2,500 |
| Paint | 1,000 |
| Carpet | 3,000 |
| **Subtotal** | **$ 7,500** |
| **Legal and accounting fees** | **$ 3,000** |
| **TOTAL** | **$39,675** |

## CheckPOINT

Why is it important to calculate your startup costs accurately?

_____

_____

# Prepare Financial Statements

Once you have prepared your list of startup costs, you are ready to begin work on financial statements, including a cash flow statement, an income statement, a balance sheet, and a personal financial statement. The first three financial statements are estimates based on how you think your business will perform in its first year. Financial statements based on projections are known as *pro forma financial statements*. The personal financial statement consists of actual figures listing your personal assets and liabilities.

## Cash Flow Statement

A *cash flow statement* describes how much cash comes in and goes out of a business over a period of time. The amount of cash coming in is your *revenue*.

The amount of cash going out is your *expenses*. The cash flow statement is important because it will show how much money you have to pay your bills.

### FORECASTED REVENUES, WALTERS ELECTRIC    January 20—

| Type of item | Quantity sold | Average price per item sold | Revenue |
|---|---|---|---|
| Halogen bulbs | 20 | $ 15 | $  300 |
| Fixtures | 12 | 200 | 2,400 |
| Outdoor light sets | 6 | 175 | 1,050 |
| Floor lamps | 3 | 150 | 450 |
| **TOTAL** | | | **$4,200** |

**Forecast Revenues**  To complete a pro forma cash flow statement, you must first forecast your revenues. When you forecast your amount of revenue, you need to analyze the demand for each of your products and services. You also need to know the prices you will charge for each item.

Felicia Walters estimates that during her first month of business she will sell 20 halogen bulbs, 12 fixtures, 6 outdoor light sets, and 3 floor lamps. To calculate her total revenues, she multiplies the quantity of each type of product she expects to sell by the price set for each item.

### FORECASTED OPERATING EXPENSES WALTERS ELECTRIC    January 20—

| Type of expense | Amount |
|---|---|
| Cost of goods | $2,400 |
| Rent | 900 |
| Utilities | 100 |
| Salaries | 2,000 |
| Advertising | 800 |
| Supplies | — |
| Insurance | 75 |
| Payroll Taxes | 175 |
| Other | 50 |
| **TOTAL** | **$6,500** |

**Forecast Operating Expenses**  Expenses incurred by a business every month are called operating expenses. They may include cost of goods (what you pay manufacturers or wholesalers to get products and services to sell), rent, salaries, payroll taxes, office supplies, utilities (electricity, telephone, water), insurance, and advertising.

**Prepare the Cash Flow Statement**  After making projections of revenues and expenses, you are ready to prepare your cash flow statement. You should create monthly pro forma cash flow statements for the first year of operation and annual statements for the second and third years to give your lender an accurate picture of your cash flow over time.

Like most business owners, Felicia knows that her operating expenses will exceed her revenues during the first few months of operation. Her cash flow will be negative because her sales will be low and some expenses will be high, as shown in the cash flow statement on the next page.

**Best and Worst Case**  Many entrepreneurs create two types of cash flow statements based on a worst-case scenario and a best-case scenario. To create a worst-case scenario cash flow statement, project lower revenues and higher expenses than you think you will really have. To create a best-case scenario, project the highest revenues and lowest expenses your business is likely to have. A worst-case scenario cash flow statement will help you identify how much cash you will need if things go worse than expected. A best-case cash flow statement will show you how much cash you will have if your business does better than expected. These scenarios will help show you and potential lenders how much cash your business is likely to generate in any situation.

**PRO FORMA CASH FLOW STATEMENT**
**WALTERS ELECTRIC**                                           **JANUARY–JUNE 20—**

| | Jan | Feb | Mar | Apr | May | June |
|---|---|---|---|---|---|---|
| Revenues | $4,200 | $4,410 | $4,410 | $4,620 | $5,775 | $6,090 |
| **Operating expenses** | | | | | | |
| Cost of goods | $2,400 | $2,520 | $2,520 | $2,640 | $3,300 | $3,480 |
| Rent | 900 | 900 | 900 | 900 | 900 | 900 |
| Utilities | 100 | 100 | 100 | 100 | 100 | 100 |
| Salaries | 2,000 | 2,000 | 2,000 | 2,000 | 2,000 | 2,000 |
| Advertising | 800 | 800 | 800 | 800 | 800 | 800 |
| Supplies | — | 15 | 30 | 50 | 50 | 50 |
| Insurance | 75 | 75 | 75 | 75 | 75 | 75 |
| Payroll taxes | 175 | 175 | 175 | 175 | 175 | 175 |
| Other | 50 | 50 | 50 | 50 | 50 | 50 |
| **Total expenses** | **$6,500** | **$6,635** | **$6,650** | **$6,790** | **$7,450** | **$7,630** |
| **CASH FLOW** | **−$2,300** | **−$2,225** | **−$2,240** | **−$2,170** | **−$1,675** | **−$1,540** |

## Income Statement

An *income statement* is a financial statement that indicates how much money a business earns or loses during a particular period. The income statement shows how much profit or loss was generated by the business. For this reason, it is also known as a *profit and loss statement*. Creating a *pro forma income statement* for a number of years will help lenders see the long-term growth projections of your business. Most businesses choose a year as the period measured by an income statement. However, some businesses choose to generate an income statement more often to view their revenues and expenses. New businesses often view their income statements monthly in order to determine whether a profit is being made.

The cash flow statement deals with actual cash coming in and going out. It shows when you actually make a payment on an invoice, or when you receive money due to you from a customer. In contrast, the income statement shows revenues you have not received and expenses you have not paid yet. It is a futuristic look at the financial stability of your business.

Suppose Walters Electric sells $5,000 worth of lighting in June. The company's monthly income statement would show income of $5,000. But Felicia may not actually have received $5,000 because customers may have paid on

**PRO FORMA INCOME STATEMENT**
**WALTERS ELECTRIC, 20—**

| Item | Year 2 | Year 3 |
|---|---|---|
| Revenues | $115,000 | $125,000 |
| **Operating expenses** | | |
| Cost of goods | $55,400 | $ 60,000 |
| Rent | 10,800 | 10,800 |
| Utilities | 1,230 | 1,260 |
| Salaries | 24,500 | 25,000 |
| Advertising | 2,205 | 2,315 |
| Supplies | 1,200 | 1,200 |
| Insurance | 600 | 615 |
| Payroll taxes | 900 | 900 |
| Other | 615 | 615 |
| **Total expenses** | **$97,450** | **$102,705** |
| **INCOME** | **$17,550** | **$ 22,295** |

credit. Felicia will not receive their payments until July or August. Also, some customers may never pay their bills. Because not all business transactions are paid for immediately, the income statement and the cash flow statement usually will be different. Customers are not the only people who defer payments. Felicia may receive $1,500 worth of merchandise to sell, but she may wait 30 days to pay the invoice. The cash flow statement will show that Felicia has the $1,500 cash she has not yet paid to her supplier. In contrast, the income statement would show that Felicia has paid the $1,500.

## Balance Sheet

Another pro forma financial statement you should prepare is a balance sheet. A *balance sheet* lists what a business owns, what it owes, and how much it is worth at a particular point in time. It does this by identifying the assets, liabilities, and owner's equity of the business. The balance sheet is based on an equation called the *accounting equation.*

$$\text{Assets} = \text{Liabilities} + \text{Owner's Equity}$$

**PRO FORMA BALANCE SHEET**
**WALTERS ELECTRIC**                    **December 31, 20—**

| Assets | | Liabilities | |
|---|---|---|---|
| *Current assets* | | *Current liabilities* | |
| Cash | $ 1,000 | Accounts payable | $12,000 |
| Accounts receivable | 8,000 | | |
| Less uncollectible accounts | −500 | *Long-term liabilities* | |
| Inventory | 14,000 | Loans payable | 17,900 |
| Total current assets | 22,500 | **Total liabilities** | **$29,900** |
| *Fixed assets* | | | |
| Equipment | 8,975 | | |
| Less depreciation | −1,795 | | |
| Furniture | 2,200 | | |
| Less depreciation | −220 | | |
| Vehicles | 18,000 | **Owner's Equity** | |
| Less depreciation | −3,600 | Felicia Walters | **$16,160** |
| Total fixed assets | 23,560 | **Total liabilities and** | |
| **Total assets** | **$46,060** | **owner's equity** | **$46,060** |

**Assets** are items of value owned by a business. They include items such as cash, equipment, and inventory. **Liabilities** are items that a business owes to others. They include loans and outstanding invoices. **Owner's equity** is the amount remaining after the value of all liabilities is subtracted from the value of all assets. It is commonly referred to as the *net worth* of the business.

This financial statement is called the balance sheet because the accounting equation must always be in balance. This means that the assets of a business always equal liabilities plus owner's equity. A business that has more assets than liabilities has positive net worth. A business that has more liabilities than assets has negative net worth.

**Types of Assets** Businesses usually separate assets into fixed assets and current assets. *Fixed assets* are assets that will be used for many years. They include buildings, furniture, and computers. *Current assets* include cash, assets that can be converted into cash, and items that are used up in normal business operations. Assets that can be converted into cash include inventory and accounts receivable. *Accounts receivable* are the amounts owed for products or services sold to customers on credit. Assets that are used up in business operations include supplies and insurance.

## Business Math Connection

Patsy Moss recently opened a mobile dog grooming business. She is preparing a balance sheet to include in her first financial statements. She adds up the value of all the property her business owns, and it equals $26,500. She has determined that she owes $15,100 on her loans for her van and equipment. What is her owner's equity?

**SOLUTION**

Use the following formula to calculate owner's equity.

Assets  &minus;  Liabilities  =  Owner's Equity

$26,500 &minus;   $15,100  =     $11,400

Patsy's owner's equity is $11,400.

**Types of Liabilities** *Long-term liabilities* are liabilities that are payable over several years. A bank loan is a type of long-term liability. *Current liabilities* are liabilities that are payable within a short amount of time, such as a utility bill and accounts payable. *Accounts payable* are the amounts a business owes to suppliers for merchandise it purchased on credit.

**Reduction in Assets** Some customers will fail to pay for the merchandise they purchased on credit. The amount a company estimates it will not receive from customers for items purchased on credit is known as the *allowance for uncollectible accounts*.

Business equipment will lose value over time. The lowering of the value of an asset to reflect its current value is **depreciation**. Estimates for uncollectible accounts and depreciation should be included on your balance sheet to ensure it provides an accurate picture of the value of your assets.

## Personal Financial Statement

Banks are usually interested in the personal financial status of the people to whom they lend money. For this reason, you will have to prepare a statement of your personal finances if you apply for a bank loan. A personal financial statement is a balance sheet showing your personal assets, liabilities, and net worth. Personal assets could include checking and savings accounts. Liabilities could include a car loan and credit card debt. Subtract your liabilities from your assets to calculate your net worth.

## CheckPOINT

What are the four financial statements you must prepare before approaching potential lenders and what does each show?

_____

_____

## Think Critically

1. Why do you think banks require so much financial information when considering lending money? Why should you provide both worst- and best-case scenarios for your pro forma cash flow statement?

_____

_____

_____

_____

_____

2. Why do you think most businesses prepare income statements on an annual basis? Why might it be helpful to an entrepreneur to view an income statement each month?

_____

_____

_____

_____

_____

## Make Academic Connections

3. **Math** The estimated startup costs for a website developer who plans to operate out of a home office are as follows: computer hardware, $4,500; computer software, $1,560; telephone system, $850; office supplies, $585; furniture and fixtures, $4,575; legal and accounting fees, $2,450. What are the total startup costs?

_____

_____

4. **Math** The website developer's total assets are $32,820 and owner's equity is $24,680. What are total liabilities? Use the accounting equation to calculate your answer.

_____

_____

5. **Math** Calculate your net worth by creating a personal financial statement. Consider savings or checking accounts you have, income from a job or allowance, fixed assets (cars, computers, furniture, etc.), and liabilities (money you owe).

### JUMP START

Frank and Jeremy decided that they needed approximately $6,000 to get their customized calendar business started. They both live with their parents and do not have to worry about living expenses. Between the two of them, they have $3,500 in savings. They thought about going to the bank for a loan, but since neither of them have any collateral and they are both under 18, they decided the bank probably would not grant them a loan. Instead, they decided to ask their family and friends for help. What do you think people would want to know before they invest in Frank and Jeremy's business?

**GOALS**

Identify different types of bank loans

Evaluate Small Business Administration and other loans

**KEY TERMS**

debt capital, p. 161
collateral, p. 161
equity capital, p. 164
venture capitalists, p. 165

## Bank Loans

Most businesses get loans from banks. You obtain debt capital when you borrow from a bank. **Debt capital** is money loaned to a business with the understanding that the money will be repaid, with interest, in a certain time period.

### Types of Bank Loans

Banks make two kinds of loans. *Secured loans* are loans backed by collateral. **Collateral** is property that the borrower forfeits if he or she defaults on the loan. Suppose you take out a $25,000 business loan and use your home as collateral. If you fail to repay the loan, the bank has the right to take ownership of your home and sell it to collect the money you owe. Banks accept different forms of collateral, including real estate, savings accounts, life insurance

**TEAMWORK**

Work in pairs and choose a business. List five reasons this business might need a short-term loan and five reasons this business might need a long-term loan. Present your results to the class.

policies, and stocks and bonds. *Unsecured loans* are loans that are not guaranteed with collateral. They are made only to the bank's most creditworthy customers and are usually paid back within a short time period.

## Types of Secured Loans

There are three kinds of secured loans: lines of credit, short-term loans, and long-term loans. A *line of credit* is an agreement by a bank to lend up to a certain amount of money whenever the borrower needs it. Banks charge a fee for extending lines of credit to their customers, whether or not money is actually borrowed. They also charge interest on borrowed funds. Most small businesses establish lines of credit to help them make purchases as necessary.

A *short-term* loan is made for a very specific purpose and is repaid within a year. Businesses use short-term loans to help with seasonal cash flow problems. A *long-term loan* is payable over a period longer than a year. Long-term loans are generally made to help a business make improvements that will boost profits.

## Reasons a Bank May Not Lend Money

Obtaining bank financing for a startup business is difficult, but it is not impossible. Banks use various guidelines to determine if borrowers are a good risk. Some of the reasons banks turn down loan applications include

1. **The business is a startup.** Banks are often reluctant to lend money to new businesses that have no record of repaying loans. They are more likely to default on their loans than companies already in business.

2. **Lack of a solid business plan.** Banks evaluate businesses based on their business plans. A company with a poorly written or poorly conceived business plan will not be able to obtain financing from a bank.

3. **Lack of adequate experience.** Banks want to be sure that people setting up or running a business know what they are doing. You have to show that you are familiar with the industry and have management experience.

4. **Lack of confidence in the borrower.** Even if your business plan looks solid and you have adequate experience, you may fail to qualify for financing if you make a bad impression on your banker. Make sure you dress and behave professionally and are on time for appointments.

5. **Inadequate investment in the business.** Banks are suspicious of entrepreneurs who do not invest their own money in their businesses, and they are unlikely to lend to them.

## CheckPOINT

What are some of the reasons banks reject loan applications?

_____

_____

# SBA and Other Loans

Sometimes you cannot obtain a bank loan. You can turn to the Small Business Administration (SBA) for assistance. The SBA is a federal government agency whose purpose is to help small businesses. In addition to providing management and technical advice, the SBA guarantees loans made by commercial banks. This means that if you default, the SBA will pay a percentage of the loan to the bank. This makes banks more willing to lend money.

When the SBA guarantees a bank loan, it asks that the money borrowed be used to buy fixed assets or as working capital. *Working capital* is the money needed to meet the day-to-day needs of a business. Working capital loans are usually for five to seven years. Fixed asset loans are for longer periods of time. The SBA can make loans directly to small businesses, but it does not have much funding available for direct loans.

## Requirements of SBA Loans

To qualify for assistance from the SBA, your company must meet certain requirements. The SBA will review your business plan and decide whether or not to help you finance your business.

1. **Your business must be considered a small business.** The definition of "small" depends on the industry. In some retail industries, a company can have sales of $27 million and still be considered small. To find out if your company qualifies for assistance, contact your district SBA office.

2. **Your business must not be the leader in its field.** If, for example, you own the most popular restaurant in your town, you will not qualify for SBA financing.

3. **Your business must comply with federal employment laws.** These include the Equal Employment Opportunity Act, Americans with Disabilities Act, OSHA regulations, Family and Medical Leave Act, and Fair Labor Standards Act.

4. **Your business cannot create or distribute ideas or opinions.** This means that newspapers, magazines, and academic schools are not eligible for SBA financing.

5. **You must have been unable to obtain financing from a commercial bank.**

6. **You must invest a reasonable amount of your own money in the venture.** Entrepreneurs usually cover 30 to 50 percent of the total cost to begin their businesses.

7. **You must provide adequate collateral.** If the assets of your business are insufficient, you must provide personal guarantees to secure financing.

In addition to the requirements your business must meet, your personal finances and experience will affect your ability to obtain financing from the SBA. You will need to show that you have a good personal credit history and have filed and paid your personal and business income taxes. You will also need to show that you have experience running your own business.

## Other Sources of Loans

Besides the SBA, there are other government agencies that make loans.

1. **Small Business Investment Companies** SBICs are licensed by the SBA to make loans to and invest capital with entrepreneurs.

2. **Minority Enterprise Small Business Investment Companies** MESBICs are special kinds of SBICs that lend money to small businesses owned by members of ethnic minorities.

3. **Department of Housing and Urban Development** HUD provides grants to cities to help improve impoverished areas. Cities use these grants to make loans to private developers, who must use the loans to finance projects in needy areas.

4. **The Economic Development Administration** The EDA is a division of the U.S. Department of Commerce that lends money to businesses that operate in and benefit economically distressed parts of the country. Borrowing from the EDA is similar to borrowing from the SBA, but the application is more complicated and the restrictions are tighter.

5. **State Governments** Government assistance may also be available at the state level. Almost all states have economic development agencies and finance authorities that make or guarantee loans to small businesses.

6. **Local and Municipal Governments** City, county, or municipal governments sometimes make small loans to local businesses. The loans are usually $10,000 or less.

Why might you apply for a business loan with a government agency?

## Applying for a Loan

To apply for a loan from the SBA or another government agency, you will need to provide your business plan, including information on the type and location of your business, the date the business started or is projected to start, and the product or service you are offering. You also should include information on your prospective customers, competition, and suppliers as well as your management experience. Finally, you will need to submit your business financial data and a description of how you plan to repay the loan, supported by financial statements. You may also be asked to provide copies of lease agreements, franchise agreements, licenses, letters of reference, partnership agreements, or articles of incorporation.

## Finance Your Business with Equity Capital

Another way to finance your business is through equity capital. **Equity capital** is money invested in return for a share of the business's profits. Entrepreneurs

### CURRENCY EXCHANGES

When selling goods internationally, an entrepreneur will have to deal with foreign currency. Currency has different names in other countries. What is referred to in the United States as the dollar is called the yen in Japan and the peso in Mexico. When a U.S. entrepreneur sells a good in another country and wants to receive payment in U.S. dollars, the currency of the country where the sale took place will have to be changed into dollars using the exchange rate. The exchange rate is the relative value of the currency of one country compared with that of another. The economic conditions of the country issuing the currency, the stability of its government, and the supply of and demand for the currency are major factors affecting its value. When there is little demand for the U.S. dollar in the money markets, its value goes down, or weakens. When the demand is high, the dollar appreciates, or strengthens.

### Think Critically

If you were going to do business with a European country, would you prefer a strong dollar or a weak dollar? Why?

may seek equity capital when they do not qualify for bank or SBA loans and are not able to finance their business out of their own savings.

**Friends and Family** Some entrepreneurs ask friends and family for the capital to start their business. If you decide to borrow money from friends or family members, clearly warn them of the risks involved in lending money to a startup business. Be sure both you and they understand exactly how much interest and principal you will pay each month. Also, specify what your obligations are to pay back the loan if your business goes bankrupt.

**Venture Capitalists** Some privately owned companies sell stock through venture capitalists. Venture capitalists are individuals or companies that make a living investing in startup companies. They are usually interested in companies that have the potential of earning hundreds of millions of dollars within a few years. Because of this, many small businesses would have trouble getting venture capitalists to invest in their company.

## CheckPOINT

Name the requirements for obtaining an SBA loan.

_____

_____

_____

## Think Critically

1. Why is a secured loan easier to obtain than an unsecured loan?

_____

_____

_____

2. Why do you think most SBA assistance is in the form of loan guarantees?

_____

_____

_____

3. What criteria do you think the Department of Housing and Urban Development (HUD) uses to grant loans to cities?

_____

_____

_____

4. What are some of the ways entrepreneurs can get equity capital?

_____

_____

_____

_____

## Make Academic Connections

5. **Math** Tisha Appleton obtained a $45,000 loan for her startup business. The SBA guaranteed 75 percent of the loan. How much has the bank risked losing if Tisha's business fails?

_____

_____

6. **Communication** Conduct a telephone interview with the manager of a local bank to find out what kinds of loans the bank offers to small businesses. Specifically, ask the manager about secured loans, unsecured loans, and SBA-backed loans. Write a one-page report on your findings.

**JUMP START**

Frank and Jeremy had been operating their calendar business, Precious Memories, for almost a year and were doing very well. Orders were coming in fast for Senior Memory calendars. Jeremy was showing his friend Amber all the money the business had made that day as they were walking to English class. He stopped at his locker to pick up his English book and decided to leave the money in the locker. After English, he came back to his locker and found that the locker door had been pried open. The money was gone! What mistakes did Jeremy make in handling the business's incoming cash?

**GOALS**

Describe ways to protect your business against theft

Determine the different types of insurance you may need for your business

**KEY TERMS**

shoplifting, p. 168

workers' compensation, p. 170

## Types of Theft

As an independent businessperson, you will face many risks, including theft. Employees or shoplifters may steal your merchandise. Burglars may break into your business and steal your equipment. People may use stolen credit cards or write checks when they don't have money in their accounts.

### Employee Theft

Most employees are hard working and honest. But there are a few who will take things, such as office supplies, fixed assets, and even money. As an entrepreneur, you need to prevent and detect employee theft and then handle it once it is detected. Some businesses, such as restaurants and retail stores, are

In small groups, develop a profile of the behavior of an employee who is likely to steal. Then brainstorm a list of suggestions regarding how an employer can take measures to ensure it hires trustworthy people.

**TEAMWORK**

more vulnerable than others. If you own such a business, you may adopt the following procedures.

1. **Prevent dishonest employees from joining your company.** Screen applicants carefully. Use a company that specializes in verifying job applicants' educational backgrounds and searching their criminal records, driver's license reports, civil court records, and credit reports.

2. **Install surveillance systems.** Often the mere knowledge that they are being recorded by a video camera deters employees from stealing.

3. **Establish a tough company policy regarding employee theft.** Make sure that all employees are aware of the policy.

4. **Be on the lookout.** Watch for cash discrepancies, missing merchandise or supplies, vehicles parked close to loading areas, and so on. Keep an eye on employees who seem to work odd hours, perform their jobs poorly, or complain unreasonably. Make inquiries if an employee has an unexplained close relationship with a supplier or customer or has a personal lifestyle that seems inconsistent with his or her salary.

## Other Types of Theft

In addition to employee theft, businesses also face the risk of loss from shoplifting, robbery, credit card fraud, and bounced checks as well as the theft of information from e-commerce websites.

**Shoplifting** The act of knowingly taking items from a business without paying is **shoplifting**. Customers shoplift millions of dollars from retailers every year. If you own a retail business, you will have to take steps to prevent or reduce shoplifting. Some of the things you can do include hiring security guards to patrol your store, installing electronic devices, such as mounted video cameras, electronic merchandise tags, and point-of-exit sensors, and posting signs indicating that you prosecute shoplifters. You should also instruct your employees to watch customers who appear suspicious, and you can ask customers to leave their shopping bags behind the counter.

**Robbery** All business owners must be aware of the possibility that their business could be robbed. You can choose a safe location for your business and install dead-bolt locks and burglar alarms. To limit losses, many businesses keep minimum cash in the cash register and leave it open when the business is closed so that, in the event of robbery, the register will not be damaged. During business hours, once a certain amount of cash is received, transfer it to a safe. Some businesses use surveillance cameras, which deter prospective robbers from

### NET Bookmark

Retail stores lose billions of dollars to shoplifters each year. Entrepreneurs must control shoplifting as much as possible. Chris E. McGoey, aka the "Crime Doctor," is a security expert who has prepared an online series of crime prevention tips. Access www.cengage.com/school/business/21biz and click on the link for Chapter 6. Read the Crime Doctor's suggestions about how to prevent shoplifting and then answer: What are the six steps a retailer should observe before detaining suspected shoplifters?

**www.cengage.com/school/business/21biz**

### TECHNOLOGY AND ANTI-THEFT SYSTEMS

With shoplifting and employee theft on the rise, many businesses are turning to technology to help prevent these crimes. The FBI helped create a database for trading notes on shoplifting suspects and their methods. Many stores rely on video surveillance systems. Minneapolis-based Target Corporation tracks video feed from its 1,700 stores at regional hubs. Video recognition software mounted over checkout registers is being used to prevent cashiers from deliberately bypassing the scanner, thus not charging the customer. Electronic sensors are being used to prevent "pushout thefts," where a shoplifter pushes a cart full of merchandise out of the store without paying. Sensors installed in the carts will lock up the shopping cart wheels if the cart does not pass through an attended checkout line. These are just a few ways technology helps prevent loss.

### THINK CRITICALLY

What are the advantages of using technology to help prevent theft?

entering the business in the first place. Be aware that you may be robbed regardless of the preventative measures you take.

**Credit Card Fraud** Business owners lose millions of dollars every year from stolen credit cards. To prevent stolen credit cards from being used, you can install an electronic credit card authorizer, which checks to see if a credit card is valid. If the card has been reported stolen or if the cardholder has exceeded the credit limit, authorization will not be granted.

**Bounced Checks** When there are insufficient funds in a checking account, a check may bounce. To minimize losses, establish a policy of accepting checks drawn on in-state banks only. Charge an additional fee if a customer writes a bad check to your business. Asking for identification, like a driver's license, can help you collect money due to you. If bad checks are a serious problem in your area, you may decide not to accept checks at all.

**E-Commerce** If your business engages in e-commerce, there are many threats to your safety and that of your customers. These threats include the theft of information by hackers, theft of credit card numbers, and invalid orders. Take precautions to ensure the safety of company and customer information.

What risks do e-commerce businesses face?

© Monkey Business Images, 2009/ Used under license from Shutterstock.com

## CheckPOINT

How can you help prevent robberies and bounced checks?

_____

_____

# Business Insurance

As a business owner, you are at risk from more than just criminal activity. A fire could destroy your building. An accident could injure an employee. A broken water pipe could ruin your inventory. You can protect yourself against some financial losses by buying insurance.

## Types of Insurance

The most important types of insurance you will need for your business include property, casualty, and life insurance and workers' compensation.

**Property Insurance** Most businesses purchase property insurance, which provides coverage for damage to buildings and the contents inside the buildings, such as furniture, fixtures, equipment, and merchandise owned by the business. It protects against normal risks, including fire, robbery, and storm damage. Property insurance does not cover floods or earthquakes.

**Casualty Insurance** To protect a business against lawsuits, buy casualty insurance. It can protect your business from having to pay damages if an accident occurs on your premises and against lawsuits claiming that a defect in the product you manufactured or sold caused bodily injury to a customer.

**Life Insurance** Insurance paid in the event the holder of the policy dies is life insurance. This is important to have so that the business owner's loans and leases are paid and do not become debts for the family.

**Workers' Compensation** All businesses are required by law to provide workers' compensation. Workers' compensation covers medical expenses incurred as a result of work-related injuries. It provides income benefits to workers who are unable to work as a result of their injuries.

**Other Insurance** Depending on your business and its location, other types of insurance that you may want to purchase include flood, business interruption, crime, and renter's insurance.

## Buy Insurance

Buying insurance can be complicated. Make a list of all the property you own and its value. Then, consider the risks you want to insure against. A good insurance agent can help you make decisions about the kind and amount of coverage you need. Remember that the agent who sells you your policy will be involved in processing your claims, so he or she should be someone you trust.

## CheckPOINT

Why should a business owner purchase property insurance?

_____

_____

# Think Critically

1. What types of behavior do you think potential shoplifters might exhibit? How can entrepreneurs protect their business from shoplifters?

_____

_____

_____

2. Tim Stanton has just opened a surf shop on the beach in South Florida. He has purchased property insurance to insure his business against normal risks to his buildings, vehicles, and other business property. Against what additional risks should he consider insuring his business?

_____

_____

_____

3. What issues should you consider in choosing an insurance agent?

_____

_____

_____

# Make Academic Connections

4. **Math** At closing time, the Old World Café's cash register totaled out at $884. The cash added up to $534, and the credit card slips equaled $237. How much of the day's proceeds are not accounted for? What reasons might explain the difference?

_____

_____

_____

5. **Problem Solving** Last year the holiday season profits at Ray's Sporting Goods were reduced significantly because of shoplifting. In small groups, brainstorm ways to approach the problem this year. Create a presentation for your class.

6. **Research** You just opened a roller skating rink in your neighborhood. Make a list of all the property you own that is used in the business operations of the skating rink. List the value next to each item. Use the Internet and other resources to determine the types of insurance you should carry as the owner of a skating rink and explain why. Take into consideration your business, your customers, and your employees.

## Chapter Summary

**6.1** **Make a Financial Plan**

A. Startup costs consist of equipment and supplies, furniture and fixtures, vehicles, remodeling, and legal, accounting, and licensing fees needed to establish a business.

B. Your financial plan will consist of startup costs and four financial statements: a cash flow statement, an income statement, a balance sheet, and a personal financial statement. All of these statements, except the personal financial statement, will be pro forma financial statements.

**6.2** **Obtain Financing for Your Business**

A. A bank may help finance your business with a secured or an unsecured loan.

B. To help new businesses that cannot obtain financing from commercial banks, the Small Business Administration (SBA) offers loan guarantees. If a bank has rejected your loan application, you may be eligible to apply for an SBA loan. Besides the SBA, there are other government agencies that may fund your business venture. You can also consider financing your business with equity capital.

**6.3** **Theft Proof and Insure Your Business**

A. Once you have found financing, you will need to think about protecting your business from theft. Shoplifting and employee theft are just some of the risks business owners face.

B. There are many types of insurance you can purchase for your business. You will have to choose an insurance agent you trust who will sell you the right insurance in the right amounts.

## Vocabulary Builder

Choose the term that best fits the definition. Write the letter of the answer in the space provided. Some terms may not be used.

_____ 1. Expenses that are incurred by a business every month

_____ 2. Money invested in a business in return for a share of its profits

_____ 3. The lowering of the value of an asset to reflect its current value

_____ 4. Items of value owned by a business

_____ 5. One-time-only expenses that are paid to establish a business

_____ 6. The act of knowingly taking items from a business without paying

_____ 7. Property that the borrower forfeits if he or she defaults on the loan

_____ 8. Individuals or companies that make a living by investing in startup companies

_____ 9. Items, such as loans, that a business owes to others

_____ 10. Money loaned to a business with the understanding that the money will be repaid, with interest, in a certain time period

a. assets
b. collateral
c. debt capital
d. depreciation
e. equity capital
f. liabilities
g. operating expenses
h. owner's equity
i. shoplifting
j. startup costs
k. venture capitalists
l. workers' compensation

# Review Concepts

**Point Your Browser**
www.cengage.com/
school/business/21biz

**11.** What financial documents do you need to prepare for a potential lender or investor to assess whether your business appears viable?

_____

_____

_____

**12.** How are startup costs different from monthly operating expenses?

_____

_____

_____

**13.** Why should you create worst-case and best-case scenario cash flow statements?

_____

_____

_____

**14.** What does an income statement show?

_____

_____

_____

**15.** What is the accounting equation?

_____

_____

**16.** Why does an entrepreneur prepare a personal financial statement?

_____

_____

_____

**17.** Why do banks demand collateral?

_____

_____

_____

**18.** What information will you need to supply when applying for an SBA loan?

_____

_____

_____

**19.** What are SBICs, and what do they do?

_____

_____

**20.** Why would an entrepreneur seek equity capital?

_____

_____

**21.** What can you do to prevent shoplifting? Credit card fraud?

_____

_____

**22.** What are some of the things that may indicate to a business owner that an employee is stealing?

_____

_____

_____

# Apply What You Learned

**23.** You want to establish an amusement park. Make a list of the startup costs. Forecast your monthly revenue and operating expenses. Create both a worst- and best-case scenario cash flow statement. List the major types of insurance needed.

**24.** If you are not applying for business loans or attracting investors to your business, do you think you still need a financial plan? Why or why not?

_____

_____

_____

**25.** What is the advantage of a line of credit versus a short-term or long-term loan? Do you think a line of credit would be more or less difficult to qualify for? Why?

_____

_____

_____

**26.** Why do you think the SBA and other government agencies are willing to take a risk on an entrepreneur when a bank will not?

_____

_____

_____

**27.** Businesses lose millions of dollars every year because of stolen credit cards and bounced checks. Why wouldn't a business owner protect him or herself by accepting only cash?

_____

_____

_____

# Make Academic Connections

**28. Math**  You own a music store that sells instruments and sheet music and provides services such as lessons and instrument repair. You owe $25,000 to instrument vendors and publishers. You have a ten-year bank loan of $50,000. Your bank account balance is $13,000; you own inventory worth $57,000, and you expect $2,000 in receivables. Fixed assets are $22,000. What are your total assets? What are your total liabilities? What is your owner's equity?

_____

_____

_____

**29. Communication**  You are applying for an SBA loan for your music store. Write a letter to the SBA that provides all of the information about your business. Elaborate on your plans for your business and how you plan to use the money. How do you plan to repay the loan?

**30. Math**  You plan on opening Rashida's Beauty Salon. You have listed your projected monthly revenues, expenses, and taxes below. Use spreadsheet software to prepare a pro forma income statement based on this information.

| Revenues | $15,000 | Insurance | $ 750 |
|---|---|---|---|
| Cost of goods | 2,550 | Rent | 1,000 |
| Supplies | 1,100 | Utilities | 650 |
| Salaries | 4,800 | Taxes | 1,050 |

**31. Problem Solving**  Create a pro forma cash flow statement to project your personal revenue and expenses over the next six-month period. Do you project a positive cash flow? If so, what will you do with the extra money? If not, how can you improve your cash flow?

**32. Economics**  Research the state of the U.S. economy today and future forecasts of the economy. Based on what you learn, predict how the economy could affect the cash flow of a new business today and in the future. What recommendations would you give to a business owner based on your predictions?

# Ethical Dilemma

**33.** You asked two of your employees to perform a physical inventory over the weekend. You are certain that there were three plasma television sets in stock prior to having the employees take inventory. However, when the inventory was completed, the list showed only two plasma television sets in stock. You checked the stockroom, and you found only two. You have always trusted your employees. What would you do? Will you confront them? If so, how will you approach them? Working with a partner, role-play the conversation you will have with the employees.

# GLOSSARY

## A

**Advertising** a paid form of communication sent out by a business about a product or service (p. 117)

**Aptitude** the ability to learn a particular kind of job (p. 14)

**Assets** items of value owned by a business (p. 158)

## B

**Board of directors** a group of people who meet several times a year to make important decisions affecting the company (p. 78)

**Bonus** a financial reward made in addition to a regular wage or salary (p. 135)

**Brainstorming** a creative problem-solving technique that involves generating a large number of fresh ideas (p. 26)

**Business broker** a person who sells businesses for a living (p. 62)

**Business plan** a written document that describes all the steps necessary to open and operate a successful business (p. 34)

## C

**Channels of distribution** routes that products and services take from the time they are produced to the time they are consumed (p. 114)

**Collateral** property that a borrower forfeits if he or she defaults on a loan (p. 161)

**Commission** a percentage of a sale paid to a salesperson that varies from month to month, depending on how much of a product or service is sold (p. 136)

**Corporation** a business with the legal rights of a person that is independent of its owners (p. 75)

**Cover letter** a letter that introduces and explains an accompanying document or set of documents (p. 45)

## D

**Debt capital** money loaned to a business with the understanding that the money will be repaid, with interest, in a certain time period (p. 161)

**Delegate** to let other people share workloads and responsibilities (p. 143)

**Depreciation** the lowering of the value of an asset to reflect its current value (p. 159)

**Direct competition** competition by a business that makes most of its money selling the same or similar products or services as another business (p. 102)

**Dividends** distributions of profits to shareholders by corporations (p. 78)

## E

**Employees** people who work for someone else (p. 5)

**Entrepreneurs** people who own, operate, and take the risk of a business venture (p. 4)

**Entrepreneurship** the process of running a business of one's own (p. 4)

**Equity capital** money invested in return for a share of the business's profits (p. 164)

**Executive summary** a short restatement of the business plan (p. 46)

## F

**Franchise** a legal agreement that gives an individual the right to market a company's products or services in a particular area (p. 67)

**Franchise fee** the fee the franchise owner pays in return for the right to run the franchise (p. 68)

## I

**Ideas** thoughts or concepts that come from creative thinking (p. 17)

**Indirect competition** competition by a business that makes only a small amount of its money selling the same or similar products or services as another business (p. 102)

## J

**Job analysis** the process of determining the tasks and sequence of tasks necessary to perform a job (p. 129)

**Job description** a written statement listing the tasks and responsibilities of a position (p. 129)

## L

**Liability** the amount owed to others (pp. 79, 158)

## M

**Market research** a system for collecting, recording, and analyzing information about customers, competitors, goods, and services (p. 92)

**Market share** a business's percentage of the total sales generated by all companies in the same market (p. 109)

**Marketing** all of the processes—planning, pricing, promoting, distributing, and selling—used to determine and satisfy the needs of customers and the company (p. 88)

**Marketing mix** a blending of the four marketing elements of product, price, distribution, and promotion used to reach a target market (p. 89)

**Marketing plan** a written plan that defines a business's market, identifies its customers and competitors, outlines a strategy for attracting and keeping customers, and identifies and anticipates change (p. 99)

**Marketing strategy** a plan that identifies how a business's goals will be achieved (p. 98)

## O

**Operating expenses** expenses incurred by a business every month (p. 156)

**Opportunities** possibilities that arise from existing conditions (p. 17)

**Organizational structure** the relationship between various jobs in an organization (p. 129)

**Owner's equity** the amount remaining after the value of all liabilities is subtracted from the value of all assets (p. 158)

## P

**Partnership** a business owned by two or more people (p. 75)

**Performance appraisal** a management control tool that helps determine whether the objectives for a particular job are being met (p. 144)

**Pro forma financial statement** financial statement based on projected revenues and expenses (p. 43)

**Problem-solving model** six steps that help people solve problems in a logical manner: (1) define problem, (2) gather information, (3) identify various solutions, (4) evaluate alternatives and select best option, (5) take action, and (6) evaluate the action (pp. 23–25)

**Product mix** the different products and services a business sells (p. 108)

**Profit sharing** a compensation arrangement in which employees are paid a portion of the company's profits (p. 136)

**Publicity** a nonpaid form of communication that calls attention to your business through media coverage (p. 120)

## R

**Recruit** to look for people to hire and attract them to your business (p. 130)

**Royalty fee** weekly or monthly payment made by the owner of a franchise to the seller of the franchise (p. 68)

## S

**Salaries** fixed payments for labor or services stated on an annual basis (p. 135)

**Self-assessment** an evaluation of one's strengths and weaknesses (p. 13)

**Service Corps of Retired Executives (SCORE)** group of retired executives who volunteer their time to provide entrepreneurs with real-world advice and know-how (p. 51)

**Share of stock** a unit of ownership in a corporation (p. 78)

**Shoplifting** the act of knowingly taking items from a business without paying for them (p. 168)

**Small Business Administration (SBA)** an independent agency of the federal government that was created to help Americans start, build, and grow businesses (p. 51)

**Small Business Development Centers (SBDC)** provides management assistance to current and prospective small business owners (p. 51)

**Sole proprietorship** a business owned exclusively by one person (p. 75)

**Startup costs** one-time-only expenses that are paid to establish a business (p. 155)

**Statement of purpose** a brief explanation of why you are asking for a loan and what you plan to do with the money (p. 46)

## T

**Target market** individuals or companies that are interested in a particular product or service and are willing and able to pay for it (p. 89)

**Trade associations** organizations made up of professionals in a specific industry (p. 52)

**Trade shows** special meetings where companies of the same or a related industry display their products (p. 19)

## V

**Valuator** an expert on determining the value of a business (p. 64)

**Venture capitalists** individuals or companies that make a living investing in startup companies (p. 165)

## W

**Wages** payments for labor or services that are made on an hourly, daily, or per-unit basis (p. 135)

**Workers' compensation** a type of insurance that covers medical expenses incurred as a result of work-related injuries (p. 170)

# INDEX